Making Life Better through Road Trips with Heather

LAURA VERREKIA

DEDICATION

This book is dedicated to my sister, Heather, who celebrates a milestone birthday this year. I thought she had reached the milestone last year, so when she told me "one more year," I realized I had time to create a special gift to show her how much she means to me. Happy Birthday, Heather.

CONTENTS

ACKNOWLEDGMENTS

Thank you to my friends who edited drafts of the book:

Kimberly Koury has been my best friend since we met in our freshman year of high school. Kim and I have taken many road trips together, so she was an ideal choice to edit this book. Some of my favorite road trips with Kim include a day spent in Cape May, New Jersey where we witnessed a marriage proposal in a lighthouse, and a hike up Hawk Mountain in Kempton, Pennsylvania. I am grateful for Kim's feedback on early drafts of this book, and I appreciate her unwavering support of me. Kim is a beautiful, intelligent, humorous, and uncommonly kind woman. Her favorite inspirational quote is:

"One day you will wake up and there won't be any more time to do the things you've always wanted to do. Do it now."

Barbara Hampel has been my aunt my whole life, but over the last few decades she has become one of my best friends. My children forget she is my aunt because we interact like peers. When I decided to write this book, I knew right away that I wanted Barbara to create an illustration for the cover. Barbara is a talented artist. At first she protested that her skills were not up to the task, but I believe the sketch she whipped up one morning while I was visiting her in Maine speaks for itself. It is on the front cover of this book. Barbara dedicates this drawing to her father, my "Grampy Joe," who also had artistic talent and would have loved to be part of this book. Barbara edited a draft of this book and was especially helpful in fact-checking my stories about Maine. Her favorite inspirational quote is:

"There's beauty where the brush does not touch."

Robert Elwood, who I affectionately refer to as "Bob the lawyer" is not actually my lawyer. Over the last few years, Bob and I have become very close as we share conversations over hikes and lunches. Although I love both the hikes and the lunches, I sometimes feel I don't need the calories or expense of the lunch. One of my favorite memories from walking and dining with Bob was a time when I wanted to skip our after-walk lunch and I expressed that to Bob. "No problem," he said, "but let's try a new trail." I was amused to find that our new trail led through a town called Manayunk, where lunch at a Greek restaurant was built right into the middle of the hike! I am immensely grateful for Bob's feedback on a draft of this book. His favorite inspirational quote is:

"Have…a good time…all the time."

Karin Hampel deserves a mention because she would have loved to edit this book. I did not give her the chance. Karin is my mother and she has been my chief editor since I was in elementary school. As I wrote this book, I would have welcomed her input, but I knew it would be too hard for her to keep the project a secret from my sister. Karin is a fantastic editor and I look forward to working with her again on a future project. Her favorite inspirational quote is:

"Let go and let God."

Thank you to my children who encourage my writing:

All three of my beautiful daughters supported me as I took road trips, taught university classes, and read countless books on positive psychology. I asked each of them to contribute their favorite inspirational quote to this book.

Bridget chose: *"It is never too late to be who you might have been."*

Jamie chose: *"Happiness is when you stop comparing yourself to other people."*

Taylor chose: *"Failure will never overtake me if my determination to succeed is strong enough."*

Thank you to the college students who have inspired me:

I have gained so much from knowing each of my students, even if our lives only crossed for a brief time. Students who took my Positive Psychology class in the Spring of 2016 tried out the techniques in this book. Students who enrolled in my Research Methods classes in the Spring of 2016 tested the quizzes for me.

Thank you to Heather for all of the road trips:

My relationship with Heather will be described throughout this book. Her favorite inspirational quote is:

"Happiness is a mouse that sits on your doorstep."

This is actually a misquote from a lyric in the Matchbox Twenty song *3am*: "Happiness is a mat that sits on her doorway." When Heather's friend misquoted the song, it created an amusing visual image that makes Heather smile.

Happiness is a road trip with your sister…

≈≈≈ INTRODUCTION

I am pacing my driveway in anticipation when Heather pulls up in her white SUV. She gives me a wave and a smile. Today, we will be driving to Connecticut to hike up a mountain I discovered when I was in college. As I climb into the car, Heather glances at me to inspect my outfit. I've dressed for hiking and brought a small bag with back up clothes and shoes in case our day takes an unexpected turn. *It will.* I see a stack of computer printouts on the console between us. Heather has found several attractions along our route. "Let's Go!" by Calvin Harris pulsates from the radio as she starts the car and we begin our journey.

Road trips take you out of your day to day life and bring you to a place where you can grow. Books like *Zen and the Art of Motorcycle Maintenance* by Robert Pirsig and *Killing Yourself to Live* by Chuck Klosterman explore the personal growth you can experience when you go out on the road with a loose plan and a sense of adventure. Movies like "Thelma and Louise" and "Sideways" reveal life lessons that can be learned when you escape your daily life and find new perspective. Even if you have never taken a road trip, you can relate to the personal growth themes in these books and movies.

Most books and movies about road trips focus on trips that span several days. However, many of the road trips I will describe in this book were completed in a single day. You don't have to go far to take a road trip. You just have to get in your car and go somewhere. For me, the difference between driving your car to a supermarket and driving your car on a road trip is that one trip is necessary while the other trip is optional. If you decide to take a drive to the supermarket just to see what adventures you can find, I would classify that as a road trip. Sometimes a road trip happens on the way to a far off destination. For example, you may need to travel in your car from Point A to Point B, but the decisions you make along the way – what route to take, where to stop – make it a road trip by my definition.

People who take road trips for pleasure realize that they are good for the soul. There are at least five reasons why this is true:

First, when you head out on a road trip, *you never know what's around the corner.* No amount of planning can predict everything and it is the surprises that will inspire a sense of wonder. For example, when my sister, Heather, wanted a picture with a giant fiberglass cowboy, we were surprised to find him standing in front of a large swap meet full of vendors. A quick stop for a photo turned into an afternoon adventure. Each booth brought new surprises.

Second, a road trip is a chance to *live in the moment*. When we discovered the swap meet, it provided a plethora of sensory experiences. As we moved from booth to booth the music changed from reggae to country to hip hop. We encountered the smells of barbecued foods and floral scented products. Vivid colors attracted us and we lingered over woven fabrics and beaded jewelry.

Third, as you drive on a road trip, *the music you play creates a soundtrack*. Dramatic movies are enhanced by a soundtrack. Your life gets a soundtrack when you take a road trip. You can select music to elicit the emotion you want to feel. On a long trip home from the beach after a holiday weekend Heather and I listened to a music playlist that my best friend Kim put together. The playlist included several dance hits from the 1980's, like Prince's "Take Me With U." Through the music, Heather and I were transported back to our youth. Prince would have been a good road trip companion as he sings, "I don't care where we go. I don't care what we do. I don't care, pretty baby, just take me with you."

Fourth, *road trips are inexpensive and require minimal planning*. Fill your tank with gas. Head out and see where the road takes you! Spontaneity is good for the soul. It is not unusual for a Sunday breakfast with Heather to turn into "Where should we drive today?"

Finally, *a road trip will provide distance from your everyday life so you can see it from a new perspective.* I have often come home from a road trip feeling differently about my life than I did when we left. One thing I realize is that I may not need the things I am clinging to in my everyday life to be happy. If there is something that is causing me stress, leaving it behind for a day makes me realize that I can survive without it and it might be time to let it go.

I don't know when I started taking road trips with my sister Heather. I think they began as practical trips with a goal in mind and somehow evolved into trips taken just for the fun of the journey. When we were children, our family drove 12 hours from our home in Pennsylvania to Old Town, Maine for Christmas every year. Heather and I, along with our sister Julie and brother Joe, were passengers on those trips. This gave us lots of time for games and other creative pursuits. I remember a lot of singing in four part harmony on those car rides. Maybe those annual trips to Maine kindled our love for road trips.

As an adult, I began to call Heather to ask if she was free when I needed to reach a destination, but didn't want to travel alone. Sometimes the goal was necessary, such as picking up my daughter from college, but often the goal was out of curiosity, like finding a bakery someone had recommended in Saint Peters Village. Not only would Heather agree to accompany me, but she would plan interesting stops along the way. For example, on the way to a destination in New Jersey, we made a quick stop at a health clinic in Delaware to take pictures with a "Huge

Doctor's Bag with Stethoscope." Soon, the journey became the destination and I was calling Heather anytime I needed an adventure.

My sister Heather is seven years younger than I am. She was my living doll as I was growing up. I could dress her up in adorable outfits and create a collection of pictures with my Polaroid camera. I choreographed dances for her. When she was seven years old I created a dance for her to the Stray Cats' song "Sexy and Seventeen." Even though she was only a little girl, she proudly flipped her hair and swung her jean jacket over her head as she moved through the dance steps I taught her. Today, she is the one who teaches me moves on the dance floor.

When we lived together as children, we were in very different stages of life. I was learning to drive a car as she was learning to ride a bike. She was only a preteen when I headed off to college. I rushed out of a class in my doctorate program to see her high school graduation. As adults we reconnected and our road trips have allowed us to create a special bond.

Heather is very creative. She loves to surprise people with thoughtful gifts. It is not uncommon for Heather's friends and relatives to find just the item they need appear at their home after a visit from Heather. Heather is also a good party planner. For Halloween, she decorates her house, prepares Halloween snacks and plans Halloween themed activities. One year, we played a game called "Don't be the first to die in the horror movie!" It was a scavenger hunt through her house, with trivia questions at each stop. When Heather plans a road trip, you can expect fun surprises. No matter where we are headed, Heather finds crazy things to see along the way, like the "World's Largest Barbell," or a "House Shaped Like a Shoe."

As adults, we are busy with our careers, homes and families. I work as a college professor and Heather works in the ever-changing field of internet technology. Road trips give us a much needed break from our daily lives. Over the years, road trips with Heather have become something that revitalizes my soul. During each drive, we talk and laugh and listen to music. At each destination, we encounter surprise and wonder. We return from each trip with crazy pictures and amazing stories. I have come to realize that these road trips help my spirit grow.

As I think about my road trips with Heather, I realize there are at least ten life lessons I have learned from these trips:

1) Coincidences can be meaningful
2) It is important to be excited about your life
3) It is okay to aim high
4) There is so much to be grateful for
5) Fear can be overcome
6) There is more than one way to get to your goal
7) People matter
8) It is important to pay attention
9) Don't waste time rushing
10) It can be a wonderful life

Throughout this book I will share some stories from the road trips I have taken with my sister Heather. Each chapter has a theme that corresponds to the 10 life lessons listed above. After reading about that theme in the road trip stories, you can take a personality quiz to assess that life lesson. For example, after reading about road trips that required a change of course, you will find a quiz that measures your own willingness to change course. There are personality quizzes for each of the ten life lessons. Although your answers to the quiz questions are fixed at the moment you take the quiz, you will find that your feelings can change as you move through your life. Don't be surprised if you pick up this book again in a few months and find that your quiz scores have changed. Maybe over time you have developed an attitude of gratitude or learned how to listen.

To help you improve your quiz scores, each chapter also includes an exercise to help you work on the life lesson from that chapter. Many of the techniques you will read about have been tested on students in my Positive Psychology class at West Chester University. Some of the exercises can be done immediately, and others will be carried out over time. Although I have arranged these chapters in an order that makes sense to me, you can take the quizzes and exercises at any time and in any order you choose. My hope is that reading this book will make your life better. I know mine has greatly improved thanks to road trips with Heather.

≈≈≈ LANTERNS ON THE BEACH AT MIDNIGHT

New Year's Eve is a night of high expectations. Although it can be a time of reflection, a time to think about the year that is ending and plan the year ahead, most of us don't spend the night sitting in quiet contemplation. People want to know "What are you *doing* New Year's Eve?" One of Heather's favorite video clips features Zooey Deschanel and Joseph Gordon Levitt singing the song "What Are You Doing New Year's Eve?"

After my marriage ended, I often found myself alone on New Year's Eve. One year, Heather offered to make some plans so we would be doing something on New Year's Eve. In true road trip fashion, she wanted to find something inexpensive that required minimal planning. Her internet searching led her to a bonfire and New Year's celebration at a church about 30 minutes away. When we arrived, it was clearly a youth group gathering. We laughed as we realized our road trip in search of something to do for New Year's Eve was just beginning. After considering and dismissing a few other possibilities, we set off for Rehoboth Beach, Delaware, which was a three hour drive. Heather had a friend who lived there who had said, "Come visit sometime." What better time than New Year's Eve?

As we drove down to Rehoboth Beach, we talked about life and listened to the radio. Heather was driving, as she often does. Whenever we start off on a road trip, Heather asks if I want to drive, but I think she prefers to drive the first part of the trip because she plans surprise stops along the way. I usually get my turn to drive on the way home. Since Heather was driving, I exchanged a few end of the year texts with friends. I was so distracted by my phone and conversations with Heather that I couldn't believe the trip had taken three hours! This drive was just what I needed. It gave me an opportunity to talk to Heather about all the changes happening in my love life at that time. I was single for the first time in 15 years and it was a little scary.

Heather's road trips remove me from my everyday life and put me in a new place where I can focus on the present and come back with a new attitude. When we arrived in Rehoboth it was almost midnight. We connected with Heather's friend and he suggested we head down to the beach to ring in the New Year. There is such pressure at midnight on New Year's Eve; I had no one to kiss! But when we arrived at the beach we saw crowds of people lighting Chinese lanterns — small hot air balloons made of paper. At the stroke of midnight they released the lanterns and the flickering lights rose up into the sky above the ocean. It was a beautiful sight! Instead of feeling like I was missing something on that New Year's Eve, I felt like I was exactly where I needed to be.

When the universe gives you just what you need that is called serendipity. Serendipity is a form of synchronicity. The concept of synchronicity was first described by Carl Jung in the 1950's. Synchronicity is when two things coincide in time in a way that is both unexpected and meaningful. It is unexpected because the two events seem to have no causal relationship. It is meaningful because the events resonate powerfully with the person who experiences the coincidence. For example, Heather and I had a desire to experience something amazing on New Year's Eve. It was simply a coincidence that we ended up on a beach filled with flying lanterns.

You might argue that even though it was a coincidence for us, it wasn't surprising that we came across something amazing on New Year's Eve because it is a night when people purposefully cause amazing things to happen. However, my road trips with Heather provided many other instances of synchronicity and I credit these road trips with increasing synchronicity in my life.

On the way home from Rehoboth Beach I exchanged a few texts with a man I had some romantic interest in. He was at a party and had been drinking. In an attempt to wish me a Happy New Year he texted "Boom...too drunk for much else." As the next song came on the car radio,

Heather laughed and said "This is your song." It was Katy Perry's song "Firework" and at first I didn't understand the connection. Then Katy sang the lyric, "Boom, boom, boom." The radio playing a song with the lyric "boom" right after the man had sent me that text saying "boom" is an example of synchronicity. Hearing the words in that song made me feel connected to him even though we were apart.

On another road trip, as Heather looked up an address of a destination to enter into her GPS, she asked me "Can you remember this street address for me?" Then she laughed when she read the address. It was 18 Brooks Road. Brooks is the last name of my college boyfriend, a man I loved who is no longer living. He was so important to my life that I chose "Brooks" as a pen name for some books I published. It seems to be some sort of sign when that name appears. It reminds me that I am still connected to him.

When we stopped at a diner on one road trip, I flipped through the menu and said, "Oh, root beer floats! They sound so delicious, except *I don't like root beer.*" I ordered an iced tea and when I took my first sip I was surprised to find I was drinking root beer! It was a strange coincidence that the waitress had brought me the wrong drink and that drink just happened to be the other drink I was thinking of as I looked at the menu. Later that same night, Heather and I stopped for drinks at a bar overlooking a beach. I looked over the menu for the island drinks and said, "Those would be delicious, but *I don't really like rum.*" Heather cautioned me to stop putting ideas into the universe that I did not want to attract into my life.

Heather's words of caution reminded me of an exercise I do in my child psychology class to teach students how ineffective it is to ask a child *not* to do something. For example, while eating dinner we might tell a child, "Don't hit your sister! Don't throw food! Stop doing that!" without specifying what we *do* want them to do. In my Developmental Psychology class, I try to get a student to sit in a chair I placed in the front of the room simply by telling that student what I don't want him to do; "Don't sit in that seat. Not that one either! Do I have to call your parents? Don't stand up. Are you trying to upset me?" The student never sits in the chair I placed at the front of the room until I say, "I would like you to come sit in the chair in the front of the room." Try this with a friend. See if you can get them to bring you an iced tea just by saying, "Don't give me root beer."

Years after my college boyfriend died, I realized I had never gone to visit his grave. When Heather and I went in search of his grave we experienced some synchronicities. Heather had gotten to know my college boyfriend when he spent time with my family during college breaks. Sadly, he committed suicide a few years after our college graduation. I still think of him often, even though he is no longer in my life. However, it had never occurred to me to visit his grave until a mutual friend sent me a picture of it over social media. I asked Heather if it might be worthwhile to make the five hour drive to his grave in Norwich, New York. I don't imagine that his spirit is tied to his grave, but I did think the trip might be a chance to share memories, and it would give us an interesting destination.

The first unexpected coincidence we experienced came when we searched for directions to the cemetery. When I entered the name of the graveyard into the computer, the address that popped up was an address for a Dunkin Donuts shop. A famous slogan from Dunkin Donuts in the 1980's, before they put one on every corner, was "It's worth the trip." I took the presence of the Dunkin Donuts at the gravesite as a sign that it would be worth it for us to make the trip to his grave.

The other synchronicity happened when we asked the radio to play a song with a message from my deceased college boyfriend. Heather and I flipped to a random station looking for a message; the lyric that played was "I don't have to be the old man inside of me." Since he died in his early twenties, he never got to be an old man. The lyric is from a song called "I Have Been Redeemed" by Big Daddy Weave. Although no one wanted to lose him, Heather and I agreed this song was fitting because he probably would argue his death had saved him, redeemed him from the pain of his life.

The presence of something unexpected and meaningful on a road trip might serve as a confirmation that you are on the right track. It might caution you to change your course. Or it might just cause you to pause and connect with the person or place that has been on your mind. When I was writing a book about a character named Jackson, I began to see the word "Jackson" everywhere on my road trips with

Heather. You'd be amazed how many Jackson Streets exist, and you'll find the name in every gift shop because it is currently the most popular baby name for boys. Each time I encountered the name "Jackson" I took it as a confirmation that I should continue my connection to the Jackson character.

Sometimes the same signs show up repeatedly. On one road trip Heather concluded that the theme was "clowns" because they seemed to show up at every place we visited. Heather told me she read that clowns project happiness and bring happiness to others when in reality the clown may be lonely and searching for something. Heather and I have both felt that we put on a happy face when we feel down, so on a visit to the Circus Town Diner in New Jersey, we could both could relate to a quote on the menu saying, "I'm with the clown!"

On the way home from that trip, I asked the radio to play a song lyric describing the theme of our trip. The radio did not play a song about clowns. The song that played was "One of These Nights" by the Eagles. That song is about anticipation. Heather and I both say "someday" we will do the things we want to do. In the meantime, these road trips allow us to express some aspects of ourselves that are waiting to come out.

When we were low on gas at the beginning of a road trip, we stopped to fill up in New Jersey. Unlike our home state of Pennsylvania, drivers are not allowed to pump their own gas in the state of New Jersey. After the attendant filled the tank we drove away. A moment later we noticed the *Maintenance Required* light was on. Heather said this has happened to her before when air got into her gas tank. We continued driving and nothing else seemed to be wrong with the car. However, when these odd events happen, you could try to find a nonliteral meaning. Heather and I use our road trips as a way to *maintain* our own sense of joy and connectedness with the world. Seeing this sign at the beginning of a road trip makes a lot of sense. Maintenance *was* required and we set off on our trip to help reset the aspects of our lives that needed attention.

When unexpected events happen, like a warning light coming on in a healthy car, it makes you stop and pay attention. When you pay attention to the present moment you are being mindful. Mindfulness is focused awareness in the present moment. Studies have found that being mindful can improve the quality of your life; mindfulness has been linked to health and psychological benefits.

One benefit of a road trip, especially if you are the driver, is that it forces you to be mindful. Ellen Langer is a scientist who studies mindfulness. She demonstrates that many of us go through life on autopilot, without really processing what is happening in the present moment. For example, she tells a story of a store clerk who realized that Langer hadn't signed the back of her credit card. When Langer signed the card and then the store receipt, the store clerk mindlessly compared the two signatures. It is standard procedure to compare the signature of the person making the purchase to the signature on the back of the card to make sure that they are the same person. However, Langer had signed the card in front of the store clerk so she already *knew* it was the same person! The signature comparison was an automated, mindless response.

I experienced autopilot one day at work when I was opening the classroom for my college students. The classroom where I teach remains locked when not in use. When I arrive at the building for class, I usually find students waiting in the lobby, so I swipe my card through a panel on the wall and unlock the door. If I have done the swipe correctly, the light on the device turns green. One day, I swiped my card several times, but I couldn't get the light to turn green. A student behind me laughed and said, "The door is already open!" Because there were students waiting in the lobby I assumed the door was locked and didn't even look at the doorway in front of me to notice the door was wide open before swiping my card.

Mindfulness is necessary for spotting synchronicity. Ellen Langer teaches people to increase mindfulness by doing things that are novel. A road trip is a great opportunity to do novel things and get out of your daily routine. Being aware of synchronicities is beneficial to your life because it leads you to opportunities you might otherwise miss. Noticing when the things you want or need show up in your life is important to help you achieve your best possible life.

Do You Experience Synchronicity?

Please rate the following statements based on your experience: N = never R = rarely S = sometimes O = often A = all the time	N	R	S	O	A
I think of calling someone, only to have that person unexpectedly call me					
I think of a product I need and ads for the product appear					
I think of a question only to have it answered by the radio, TV, or people before I can ask it					
I think of an idea and hear or see it on radio, TV or internet					
I think of someone and that person unexpectedly shows up					
As I am wondering how I will make a payment, some unexpected money appears					

	N	R	S	O	A
During a conversation, by coincidence, I see or hear a word related to the topic					
I need something and the need is met without my having to do anything					
I experience a sense of sadness and later learn I lost something or someone I love at that moment					
I am watching a movie and the plot seems to mirror my life or current situation					
I pull into a crowded parking lot and find a space opens up right in front of me					
A word or number seems to show up repeatedly					

To score this quiz :

Never=1, Rarely=2, Sometimes=3, Often=4, All the Time=5

Add up the boxes you checked to get a total score.

Now rate your experience with synchronicity:

If you scored:

above 50: You are extremely sensitive to synchronicity. This means you are aware of these meaningful coincidences occurring in your life. You are probably a person who appreciates the magic in your life.

45-49: You are very sensitive to synchronicity. This means you are often aware of these events occurring in your life. They may still catch you by surprise and induce a feeling of wonder.

40-44: You are sensitive to synchronicity. This means you do experience meaningful coincidences. You can increase this experience even further by being aware of what you are hoping for and noticing what shows up in your life.

35-39: You have an average level of synchronicity in your life. Meaningful coincidences occur in your life. You may not have been aware this was synchronicity before reading this chapter.

30-34: You are insensitive to synchronicity. You have infrequent experiences with meaningful coincidence.

25-29: You are very insensitive to synchronicity. This means you don't experience meaningful coincidences very often. You can increase this experience by understanding what synchronicity is and looking for it in the future.

below 25: You are extremely insensitive to synchronicity. You may be blocking these coincidences when you assume they are impossible.

Exercise 1: Increasing Synchronicity in Your Life

Simply taking the synchronicity quiz may have made you more aware of how often these meaningful coincidences happen in your life. The ways to increase the experience of synchronicity are to:

1) increase your awareness of synchronicity
2) make yourself available to the opportunities

To achieve Step 1, review the examples of synchronicity in the above and see if you can come up with some of your own examples of amazing timing that have occurred in your own life. For example, when I needed a wonderful New Year's Eve experience, I encountered lanterns on the beach. Or when I was thinking of my friend Kim, I passed a restaurant called Kim Sushi.

For Step 2, make yourself open to these types of coincidence. Sometimes we block them without realizing it. For example, if I drive to the mall the day before Christmas, I might assume that all of the spots will be taken and park my car several blocks away from the mall. If I had not made this assumption, I would continue to drive toward the mall and might be surprised as a car pulls out from a spot close to the mall, freeing it for me. The synchronicity would be the appearance of a great parking spot just at the moment I needed one.

People who experience a lot of synchronicity consider themselves to be lucky. Richard Wiseman, a Professor of the Public Understanding of Psychology at the University of Hertfordshire in England, has done research demonstrating that people who believe they are lucky are really just people who are optimistic and pay attention. In one study, Wiseman asked people to self-report whether they were generally "lucky" or "unlucky." Then he asked both groups to count pictures in a newspaper as quickly as possible. The task was to flip through a newspaper, count the pictures, and return the newspaper to Dr. Wiseman when they completed the task. Wiseman found that lucky people returned the newspaper significantly faster than people who believed they were unlucky. The interesting finding is *why* the "lucky" people finished so quickly. Buried within the magazine, Wiseman had placed an advertisement that told people to return the newspaper immediately and receive a monetary reward. "Unlucky" people were so busy counting the pictures that they never saw the offer. "Lucky" people, who are mindful of their situations, are more likely to see an opportunity.

In Wiseman's book, *The Luck Factor*, he identified four things that people can do to increase luck in their lives:

First, luck is increased by noticing and acting upon chance opportunities. Paying attention to what is going on around you and saying yes to new experiences can lead to more luck.

Second, listening to your intuition can increase your luck. Meditating, or using other techniques to get in touch with what you really want, can increase the chance that you will be lucky enough to stumble across just what you desire.

Third, believing that you are lucky will actually increase your luck. If you are optimistic and believe that things will turn out in your favor, you are more likely to take chances that will lead to good luck.

Finally, finding the positive side of a negative outcome increases your luck. When you reframe a bad situation to see how it turned out for the best, you will conclude that the bad event was actually very fortunate.

Making yourself aware of the things you need or desire in your life can help to achieve them. One way to make yourself aware of these things is to create a vision board. The key to a successful vision board is that it must reflect your personal desires rather than including a generic set of things that everyone is *supposed* to want. Everyone is supposed to want money and fancy possessions, but maybe what you really want is more time with your kids or a new garden hose. The one time I created a truly successful vision board, I followed these steps:

1) Choose a couple of your favorite magazines, ones you enjoy.

2) Flip through the pages of the magazines and note any words or images that you are drawn to. For example, when I did the exercise, I found myself stopping to look at pictures of lakes and blueberries or reading the words, "my favorite professor."

3) Cut out the images you were attracted to and use them to create your vision board.

4) Most vision board instructions recommend that you paste the images onto a poster board and put the board in a place where you will be greeted with the images daily. I ended up putting my magazine clippings in a clear sandwich bag and pulling them out to share with anyone who was interested.

5) If you have done this correctly, you have surrounded yourself with images of things you love and want more of in your life. The idea is that now you know…how much you like blueberries, for example… and you will be more aware of opportunities to bring the things you desire into your life.

When you do this exercise you will be attracting more meaningful coincidence into your life because now you know what to look for.

≈≈≈ RURAL ROUTE 4

As Heather and I set out on our road trips, we are often in pursuit of something. It isn't always a tangible thing. For me, it is often closure. I feel the need for a road trip when I am ending a relationship or contemplating a job change. Heather is probably seeking adventure and a change of scenery. She works hard in the field of computer technology and often spends long hours in front of a screen or meeting with her coworkers. Recently she was promoted to a management position, so now she is also responsible for training and motivation. We both love the stories we can tell when we return from a road trip, and the laughter we share on the journey. It feels good to pursue the things that give you passion or make you happy.

One time we took a trip to the Pocono Mountains with multiple goals in mind. We like to hike. There is a park there called Bushkill Falls we wanted to visit. Based on what we had read about the park, we knew we would find walking trails, waterfalls, and beautiful views. Heather and I hiked for hours at Bushkill Falls that day. Although we knew there would be trails, we hadn't anticipated all of the staircases going up and down along the waterfalls. Hiking in that park is an excellent workout.

The other thing I wanted to find on this trip was insight into a new friend of mine. I wanted to drive through his hometown to get a better sense of who he was. He told me he grew up on Rural Route 4, but he said it was hard to find. Even the mail carrier had trouble finding his house. Heather is a wizard at finding locations using the internet. For example, when she heard a coworker say that someone should "stick it where the sun don't shine," she used her computer to determine that location is Mayfield, Nebraska. Heather and I both love to explore new places, so I was sure we were up for the challenge.

Heather and I also enjoy good food, so we stopped in at Petrizzo's Italian American Restaurant near the falls and enjoyed some wine and pasta. We also like to hear live music. John, the owner of Petrizzo's assured us that if we returned later in the evening a band would be playing. He gave us his personal guitar pick and said he hoped we'd be back. Hours later, we were checking into a hotel about an hour away, so we did not make it back for the music that night.

After spending the night in a cheap motel, we began our quest to find Rural Route 4. An internet search showed us Routes 2, 3, and 5, but we couldn't find a Rural Route 4. We asked the young man at the hotel's front desk if he knew how we could find Rural Route 4, but he shook his head. We figured it would probably be near Routes 3 and 5, so we set out driving. We found lots of rural roads, but we never found Rural Route 4.

Sometimes you don't reach your destination. That is when you realize that the important thing is the journey, not the destination. My friend Randy says, "A road trip is not a destination vacation. The destination is the journey." The same thing seems to be true with happiness and pursuing your goals. Researcher, author, and speaker, Shawn Achor says, "Happiness is the joy we feel striving after our potential." Just like the pleasure in a road trip, our happiness in life comes from the journey, not the destination.

When we take a road trip, Heather comes prepared with a list of attractions, oddities, and photo opportunities. I usually bring an activity focus, such as taking a hike, seeing a new town, eating delicious food, hearing live music, or finding a beautiful view. Heather finds a way to meet my activity goals and find her list of attractions with an internet search engine. Somehow we combine our goals and create a trip that allows us both to explore our passions.

Passion is essential. It is the drive that gets us through life. Heather is passionate about making other people's lives better and that motivates everything she does. I am passionate about learning new things and connecting with other people. We use the time on our road trips to tap into our shared passions for food, music, and beauty in the world.

Heather and I share a passion for good food and wine. We have toured several vineyards on the East Coast of the United States. Many counties in Pennsylvania have wine trails that list vineyards in the area allowing you to follow a trail of vineyards, seeing beautiful locations and sampling delicious wines. When we followed the Chester County Wine Trail and visited the Black Walnut Winery, we sampled several wines and ended up selecting a delicious Syrah. While many of the vineyards we visited have rustic tasting rooms, the tasting room at the Black Walnut Winery is very elegant, so sampling wine there was a very pleasant experience.

We found our favorite vineyard store at the Manatawny Creek Winery in Pennsylvania; it is full of personal touches from the owners. We enjoyed exploring the shop, reading all the clever quotes on t-shirts like *"A good man can make you feel sexy, strong and able to take on the world. Oh, sorry…that's wine…wine does that."* and other novelty items. We ended up purchasing a Sangria with pictures of the owner's dogs on the label. We enjoyed the scenery at the Rockbridge Vineyard in Virginia. This vineyard is near the Shenandoah Valley, a place close to Heather's heart because she went to college nearby.

Heather and I share a passion for music and dancing. I have many friends who are in bands and have produced albums, so I often share their music with Heather on our road trips. A college friend of mine, Ed, still plays with his rock group *Disband* and although we have not heard them play live, we do have dinner with Ed whenever his music brings him to Philadelphia. A former student of mine started an alternative band called *Your Ghost* and Heather and I have attended some of their shows. Heather creates playlists of songs we enjoy and brings them along on our road trips. These often include dance songs from the 80's through today. Passing cars may see us car dancing to the beat as we travel to our next destination. We also like to take our chances and listen to whatever happens to be playing on the radio in a town as we pass through. Being open to new things is a great way to generate synchronicity and to increase opportunities in your life.

Heather and I share a passion for beautiful places. She sends me pictures and videos of beautiful places that are located far, far away, and then she tries to find something similar within a day's drive from our home. For example, she is currently planning us a trip to "The Grand Canyon of Pennsylvania." Most of our hiking trips involve beautiful scenery. There is something magical about climbing to the highest peak and looking out over the town, forest, or river. Some of the places we have enjoyed hiking include The Devil's Hopyard in Connecticut, Bushkill Falls in Pennsylvania, St. Peters Village in Pennsylvania, Monticello in Virginia, and Acadia National Park in Maine.

On our road trips we talk about the things we are passionate about. We often talk about our careers and our personal relationships. We use the time to explore the things we love about our jobs and friends and brainstorm about ways to bring more of what we love into our lives.

My job allows me a lot of creative freedom, although it does not provide financial security. Heather's job is financially rewarding, but she is limited in the ways she can use her creative gifts. On our road trips we can consider ways to make the best of our friendships and job opportunities to create the lives we want to live.

Heather enjoys planning our road trips. She researches unique destinations and enjoys capturing absurd moments in photographs. I've often asked her why she doesn't turn her passion for these road trips into a career. She always says, "someday." I am very passionate about my current career as a college professor, but if her "someday" ever comes, I would love to be a part of the unique road trip business she could create.

Are You Passionate About Your Life?

	SD	D	Not Sure	A	SA
Please rate the following statements based on your experience: SD = Strongly Disagree D = Disagree A = Agree SA = Strongly Agree					
I have a special talent, something I am really good at					
I really enjoy spending time with my friends					
I look forward to waking up each morning					
I have a hobby I enjoy					
I like my job					
I have clear goals I want to achieve					
I love to experience new things					
I have a sense of purpose					
I spend most of my time doing things I enjoy					
I like to share the things I care about with others					
I learn something new every day					
My life is amazing					

To score this quiz :

SD =1, D =2, Not Sure =3, A =4, SA =5

Add up the boxes you checked to get a total score.

Now rate your passion for life:

If you scored:

above 50: You are extremely passionate about your life. Having things you are passionate about brings a sense of purpose to your life.

45-49: You are very passionate about your life. You know what you enjoy and you spend time doing those things.

40-44: You are passionate about your life. You get enjoyment from many activities in your life. You should find ways to do more of these things.

35-39: You have an average level of passion for your life. Increasing the passion for your life could increase your overall happiness.

30-34: You are not passionate about your life. You would like to be more passionate about your life. You need to take some time to explore new activities and find things you enjoy.

25-29: You are lacking passion for life. This means you are not feeling inspired by the people and activities that fill your time. It is definitely time to try something new. Take a road trip!

below 25: Your life is void of passion. You are not enjoying the life you live. It is time to make a change. Start by calling a friend and asking them to help find things that will make you feel inspired again.

Exercise 2: Increasing Passion for Your Life

After taking the passion quiz you know how excited you are about the life you are living. If you aren't as excited about your life as you would like to be, the following exercise may help to increase the passion you feel for your life. Author and life coach Elizabeth Gilbert argues that we put a lot of pressure on ourselves when we hope to find a single passion, or a purpose in life. She says that passion can be fleeting. Instead, she recommends that we follow our curiosities, which may lead us to passion, or at least keep us interested along the way.

Exploring the things that you are curious about may be one way to bring more passion into your life. Take a moment and list **five things that you are curious about**. You can start each statement with "I wonder…"

1. _____
2. _____
3. _____
4. _____
5. _____

Now think about how your life might change if you went off in pursuit of the answers to those questions. For example, "I wonder if my soul mate lives in Boston," could lead to a trip to that city. You may or may not find your soul mate on that trip, but chances are good that you will find some opportunities to enhance your life that you hadn't even expected.

Another way to get in touch with the things that you are really passionate about is to remind yourself of your own mortality. Viktor Frankl, a Holocaust survivor, says that knowing we won't live forever is what motivates us to find meaning in our lives *now*. Carnegie Mellon University has a tradition of allowing professors to give a hypothetical "last lecture." Professors imagine this is the last lecture they will ever give, and it forces them to think about what is really important. For Randy Pausch, a professor in the computer science department, it really was his last lecture because he was dying from a rapidly spreading cancer. His "Last Lecture" can be seen online and has also been published as a book. In this lecture, he chose to tell students about the importance of childhood dreams and other life lessons he learned. Three main pieces of advice he gave included:

1) You only regret the things you don't do
2) Find your passion and follow it
3) People are the most important thing

Of course, you can't really live like you are dying because the money will run out and you also might burn bridges you'll need while you are alive. However, imagining that you have limited time can help you to focus on the things in your life that bring you joy. As you allow yourself to pay more attention to these things in your life, you will be more passionate about your life.

Try this exercise:

1) Imagine that you have just learned these are the last 30 days of your life.

2) Write down five things you would STOP doing immediately.

3) Describe five things you feel you NEED TO DO before you die. If this is hard, go back to the things you are curious about and see if they lead you to some goals.

4) Why are these five things worthy of your precious time? (note: if they are not worth your time, then cross them off the list)

5) Now ask yourself if there is a way you could actually spend more time doing these things in the next 30 days. In the next 60 days? In the current year? If there is something that requires planning, start planning now. Working toward the goal will bring passion into your life.

When my three teenage daughters completed this exercise their answers looked like this:

The 18-year old said she would STOP:
    1) going to school
    2) sleeping in
    3) waiting for people to contact her
    4) watching television
    5) worrying about money

She would START:
    1) traveling
    2) spending time with people she cares about
    3) eating random foods
    4) meeting Harry Styles (a pop singer)
    5) appreciating what she has

The 17-year-old said she would STOP:
    1) watching Netflix
    2) going to band practice
    3) looking at her iPhone
    4) worrying about what she wears
    5) planning her future

She would START:
    1) eating unhealthy foods
    2) writing a book
    3) traveling
    4) going to Taylor Swift concerts

5) dancing more

The 14-year old said she would STOP:
1) going to school
2) going on Instagram
3) taking showers
4) seeing relatives she doesn't like
5) waking up early

She would START:
1) jumping off waterfalls
2) seeing friends more
3) helping someone
4) getting over her fear of dogs
5) going back to Maine

You may find that some of your answers are generic, like "stop paying bills" and "spend more time with people I love." But you will also find that some answers are specific to you, like "jump off a waterfall" or "meet Harry Styles." Focusing on these specific things can help you to spend more time doing things that you are passionate about. After doing this exercise with my kids, I realized that we miss spending time with our relatives in Maine. It is a twelve hour drive for us to get there from our home and many of our relatives are no longer there, so it has been a while since we have made that trip. This exercise made us realize that we need to plan a road trip to Maine.

≈≈≈ A GIANT PIRATE

On the way home from a road trip to the Pocono Mountains, Heather and I stopped to see a giant peg-legged pirate statue at a waterpark in Breinigsville, Pennsylvania. The pirate stood alone outside the closed gate of the water park because the summer season was over. As we were taking pictures of ourselves with the pirate, who stood multiple stories high, the owner of the park drove by. He was there to do some routine off-season maintenance. He stopped to say hello and Heather told him that his pirate had been mentioned in a guidebook listing oddities in Pennsylvania. The owner had no idea it had been featured in this guide. It was as if it hadn't even occurred to him that his pirate might be of interest and draw people to his park. He asked us to take some pictures of him with his pirate, which we did.

Many of Heather's road trips involve finding large oddities. On a road trip through New Jersey, we stopped to see a Giant Cowboy who draws attention to the Cowtown

Rodeo and Farmer's Market. I had driven by this giant figure many times when I used to commute from Maryland to the Jersey Shore with my kids in the summer, but I had never stopped at that location. Heather and I took pictures with the large cowboy and his cow and we even spent time exploring the market. In the market we experienced a synchronicity when a vendor seemed to know what video we were looking for before we mentioned it. In the car we had been talking about the movie, "Revenge of the Nerds" and that was the movie the vendor suggested.

At a gas station in New Jersey, Heather found a Giant Gorilla. Her camera was not working well that day, so the picture shows a giant looming figure above us, but most of the picture is unclear. For some reason, I remember the conversation we were having as we were trying to find a way to prop the camera up somewhere so we could both jump into the picture.

Heather was telling me about a job opening at her company. She knew I was frustrated by some things that had been happening at my current place of employment. The job she described would involve training staff at a residential school for children with special needs. This would be a dramatic shift in the type of teaching I was doing, but I would still face the challenge of motivating my students. I did not apply for the job, but I was really touched by the fact that Heather knew enough about my current situation and the things that matter to me to suggest another line of work for me.

On other road trips, Heather has asked me to pose next

to a giant medical bag, a giant barbell, and a shoe the size of a house. Many road trip movies involve a stop to see a giant oddity. In *National Lampoon's Vacation*, Clark Griswold encourages his family to visit the World's Largest Ball of Twine. In *Pee-Wee's Big Adventure*, Pee-Wee Herman visits a giant dinosaur attraction. Giant oddities are interesting because they grab your attention.

On the way to Gettysburg, Pennsylvania, Heather and I stopped to take a picture with a Giant Cow outside the Turkey Hill ice cream factory. At the Turkey Hill Ice Cream Experience, you can tour the facility, taste samples, and even design your own ice cream flavor. We didn't sample the ice cream that day, but we did take pictures with the cow. Heather also planned a photo shoot with other giant ceramic animals, like pigs and lions, that she found outside of a bakery in New Jersey. These oddities get attention because they are big.

Maybe big oddities are more attractive because they are easier to find than small ones. Heather and I were never able to find a "Tiny Church" even though we drove all around the neighborhood where it was supposed to be located. The pictures of the church we saw online showed a small building that a person could walk into, but it must have been relocated because we never saw a tiny church. We did find the big oddities she planned for our trips, so they were effective in drawing us to those destinations.

Magnifying your own strengths and putting them on display can help to improve the quality of your life. Martin Seligman, the "Father of Positive Psychology," and the late

Christopher Peterson identified 24 character strengths that people value. These strengths are:

Appreciation of Beauty	Kindness
Bravery	Leadership
Creativity	Love
Curiosity	Love of Learning
Fairness	Perseverance
Forgiveness	Perspective
Gratitude	Prudence
Honesty	Self-regulation
Hope	Social Intelligence
Humility	Spirituality
Humor	Teamwork
Judgement	Zest

To qualify as a character strength, the virtue had to be a positive characteristic that was universally desirable and when displayed did not diminish another person. For example, my Love of Learning can enhance my life without detracting from the quality of your life. If you visit the University of Pennsylvania's Authentic Happiness website you can complete a questionnaire called the VIA (virtues in action) that will rank your personal strengths.

When I took the survey, my five highest strengths were Gratitude, Curiosity, Love of Learning, Leadership, and Forgiveness. I do think those traits are representative of me, and I also believe some of the traits where I ranked lower, like Humility, could use some improvement.

Heather's highest strengths were Gratitude, Humility, Humor, Fairness, and Kindness. I have seen her exhibit all of these traits on our road trips, and in everyday life. Of all the traits on the VIA, the one that correlates the most with life satisfaction is Gratitude. You will find that taking road trips can enhance your appreciation for everything in your life.

When you identify your greatest strengths you should find ways to display those strengths. If you are courageous, put yourself in situations that require courage. If you have high social intelligence make sure your job involves working with people. In the previous chapter of this book, you identified some things that you are passionate about. When you start to realize what you want to do with your life, it can be scary to think about leaving the comfort of the life you know to pursue your dreams, but you can't grow big if you are thinking small. Every one of us owns a giant pirate, that is a trait we could magnify to improve the quality of our lives. Don't leave your giant pirate standing by closed gates. Use him to draw attention to yourself and your big dreams.

Do You Dream Big?

Please rate the following statements based on your experience:

SD = Strongly Disagree   D = Disagree   A = Agree   SA = Strongly Agree

	SD	D	Not Sure	A	SA
I will achieve great wealth					
I will find lasting romantic love					
I will inspire others					
I will maintain my physical health					
I have a clear plan for my life					
I can be a leader					
I have many creative ideas					
I can have my dream career					
I can be my own boss					
I can find time for all of the things I enjoy					
I will achieve a sense of peace					
I will change the world					

To score this quiz :

SD =1, D =2, Not Sure =3, A =4, SA =5

Add up the boxes you checked to get a total score.

Now rate the size of your dreams:

If you scored:

above 50: You have extremely big dreams. You know you are an important component of this universe. Your dreams matter and you will do everything in your power to make them come true.

 45-49: You have very big dreams. You know what you want to achieve and you have the confidence needed to make your dreams come true.

40-44: You have big dreams. You know what you want and you understand that you can make these dreams come true.

35-39: You have average sized dreams. You want to make your dreams come true and you are cautiously optimistic.

30-34: You have small dreams. You have dreams but you are lacking the confidence you need to live those dreams to their fullest potential.

25-29: You have very small dreams. This means you aren't really sure what you want and you may not have the confidence to pursue what you want.

below 25: You have extremely small dreams. Your apathy is troubling. You need to take some time to think about what you want for your life and do some exercises to increase your confidence.

Exercise 3: Recognizing Multiple Possibilities

As you took the dreaming big quiz, you probably realized that dreaming big requires confidence. To chase your big dreams you need:

> 1) to know what your dream is
> 2) the confidence to pursue your dream

A dream is a vision of something you would like to achieve. One way to start identifying your dreams is to give yourself an infusion of confidence. To identify dreams, life coaches will often ask, "What would you do if you knew you could not fail?" So, take a minute and ask yourself that question:

What would you do if you knew you could not fail?

1) Imagine doing something you think is "too big" for you to achieve. Write down that goal. For example, I have always wanted to *publish a book*, but I did not feel confident that I had something worth sharing that people would want to read.

2) What are the possible outcomes if you try to make your dream come true? List all of the outcomes you can

imagine. For example, if I want to publish a book I might 1) *publish a book everyone loves*, 2) *publish a book no one likes*, 3) *publish a book no one notices*, 4) *not publish the book I wrote*, 5) *never write the book*, 6) *spend my life wishing I wrote a book*, 7) *stop wanting to write a book*. Try to list at least four possible outcomes that might result if you try to achieve your dream.

3) Now look at the possibilities you have listed and ask yourself what would be the "best possible outcome" for you. Then ask yourself why you think this would be the best possible outcome.

4) Go back to your list of outcomes, the ones that you did not rate as the best. For each of these other outcomes, imagine the best possible thing that could happen to you if this was the outcome. For example, if I *did not publish the book I wrote*, it could be that my ideas need more time to develop. Then the best possible outcome could be that years later I publish an even better book.

Once you have completed this exercise for every outcome you listed, you will realize that no matter what happens you can still achieve a "best possible outcome." Do the hard work you need to do to achieve your goal, but also trust that there are many different routes to the destination.

Theories from quantum physics suggest there are multiple possible outcomes to an event and we cannot know which one is true until we have observed it. For example, when you roll a die, it could land on 1, 2, 3, 4, 5, or 6, and you don't know the number you have rolled until you see it on the die.

Unfortunately, people often limit their possible outcomes by making assumptions. What we are doing is equivalent to rolling a die and assuming it could never come up with an even number. A fair die gives an equal chance for each outcome. In reality, life situations have some outcomes that are more likely than others. Just because something is unlikely, does not mean it is impossible.

Viktor Frankl, an Austrian scientist and Holocaust survivor says he knew when he was in a concentration camp that his chance of survival was low. Despite the odds, he decided that the outcome was unknown, and as long as surviving was a possibility he was going to live as if he would survive. This may have affected his behaviors and become a self-fulfilling prophesy.

One time when I locked my keys in my school office, I didn't realize I had left them there in the morning until I arrived at my car on the other side of campus at the end of the day. As I stood by my car I realized I had no keys to unlock it. My first thought was that my keys were locked inside my office and I would have no way to open or drive my car. I would need to call someone to drive me home. I also believed I would need to find someone with a master key to get into my office. That line of thinking rules out the possibility that my office door could be unlocked and I could walk across campus and retrieve my keys. Since I share the office with another professor, and the school day was over, finding an open door was an unlikely possibility. But it was still a possibility.

So, I headed toward my office, repeating the mantra "Best Possible Outcome." When I arrived at the office I found that simply by coincidence, the other professor had left the door closed, but unlocked. I was able to walk right in and get my keys! When you limit your outcomes, you may miss an amazing coincidence.

≈≈≈ WHEN IT RAINS, EAT CHEESE
OR GET UNDER AN UMBRELLA

One memorable road trip Heather and I took was a college tour in Virginia with my oldest daughter, who was 17 at the time. Heather attended the University of Virginia in Charlottesville so we started there. The University of Virginia has a beautiful campus with a rich history. The central lawn proceeding down from the Rotunda is lined with residences for an academic village designed by Thomas Jefferson. One of Heather's favorite places on campus is the Whispering Wall at Hume Fountain. Heather showed my daughter how a person could whisper something at one end of the curved stone wall and it would be heard by a person standing by the other end of the wall. As we sat through the college admission information session and heard the requirements for acceptance at the University of Virginia, Heather turned to me and whispered, "Wow, I will never get in here...oh, wait, I have already graduated!"

We also visited the College of William and Mary in Williamsburg, Virginia. All three of us loved the historic town. Even though it was a rainy summer day when we visited, we enjoyed the food and gift shops. My daughter especially loved the local cheese shop. We sampled sandwiches and cookies, and marveled at the large wine cellar. Although the sky was overcast, we decided to eat our sandwiches on the patio outside the shop. All of a sudden, rain began to pour down from the sky. Heather and I huddled under an umbrella at an outdoor table. When we noticed that my daughter was not with us under the umbrella we looked at the cheese shop and saw her waving and smiling from the window. She had dashed inside when the rain began. Heather and I had chosen to shelter in place, while my daughter had abandoned her lunch and moved to drier ground. People react differently when faced with challenges.

How we react to a negative situation can be influenced by our attributional style. Attributional style refers to how we attribute blame or credit to life events. For example, if a student fails an exam, she will look for an explanation for that event. The student could conclude that she failed the exam because she didn't study or she could conclude that she failed the exam because the test was too hard. These two explanations place the blame for the failure in different places. Psychologists have found that people can attribute the cause of an event internally (give credit or blame to themselves) or externally (give credit or blame outside themselves). Sometimes people believe the cause of the event is temporary and sometimes they believe the cause of the event is permanent. The student who believes she failed a test because she didn't study should see that this does not have to be a permanent issue. Finally, the cause of an event can be attributed locally or globally. If the cause is local, then the event was caused by something specifically related to that event. If the cause is global, then it is pervasive and can affect other events as well. For example, the student may believe "this test was hard" (local) or "all tests are hard" (global).

Giving Credit for Success and Failure

	Optimist	Pessimist
Success	internal permanent global	external temporary local
Failure	external temporary local	internal permanent global

Researchers have found that certain attributional styles are associated with optimism and pessimism. People who attribute *success* to internal, permanent, global factors and who attribute *failure* to external, temporary, local factors tend to be optimists. People who show the opposite pattern tend to be pessimists. You could argue that Heather and I showed optimism when we stayed outside during the rain storm. We knew eventually the storm would pass and we could resume our lunch on the cheese shop patio. When we face challenges on our road trips, like rain, or oddities that seem to vanish right before we arrive at the destination, we find an opportunity to practice optimism. For example, when we failed to find the Tiny Church, we assumed someone must have moved it (external), we knew this was a temporary setback in our day, and we continued to search for the next oddity because we did not believe the problem was global or pervasive.

One of my favorite quotes is, "You can have everything you want the moment you want everything you have." I have often found this to be true. In my first experience creating a vision board, I realized that I had everything on the board except the fancy workout sneakers. When I bought the sneakers, I had everything I had requested from the universe. When my friend Rod was helping me brainstorm ideas for a new career, he asked me to describe the kinds of things I would be doing in my ideal job. I said I would like to work with intelligent people, I wanted to be able to share my ideas, and I wanted to influence people's lives. Rod smiled and pointed out that my current job as a professor allowed me to do all of those things. I had only been focusing on the frustrating things about my job. When I switched my attention to the positive aspects, an immediate job change no longer seemed necessary.

Every road trip I take with Heather fills me with

gratitude. I am grateful that I can find time to escape my daily stresses. I am grateful that I have a car to take me to these destinations. I am grateful that I have a sister who will spend time with me. I am grateful that I am healthy enough to climb mountains. I am grateful for the joy I experience when Heather shows me a local wonder that surprises me. I am grateful for the delicious food and drink we sample on our trips. I am grateful for the wonder of nature when we walk along a creek or see a beautiful sunset. There is so much to be grateful for on a road trip, and in life.

Are You Grateful?

Please rate the following statements based on your experience:

N = never   R = rarely   S = sometimes   O = often   A = all the time

	N	R	S	O	A
Good things happen to me					
I appreciate my friends					
I feel fortunate to have my current job					
I am thankful for the home where I live					
Other people have helped me to achieve my goals					
I see setbacks as learning experiences					
I am blessed to experience the beauty of the world around me					
I am glad that I am me and not someone else					
I give thanks when I have sufficient resources (food, water, money, etc.)					
I appreciate the freedom to make my own decisions					

	N	R	S	O	A
I am happy with what I have achieved in life so far					
I am grateful for new opportunities to learn and grow					

To score this quiz :

Never=1, Rarely=2, Sometimes=3, Often=4, All the Time=5

Add up the boxes you checked to get a total score.

Now rate your level of gratitude:

If you scored:

above 50: You are extremely grateful. You appreciate the gifts in your life.

45-49: You are very grateful. You know you are surrounded by positive things.

40-44: You are grateful. You are starting to realize that you have some very good things in your life.

35-39: You have an average level of gratitude. This can improve if you start to notice the positive things in your life.

30-34: You are not feeling gratitude. You need to learn to appreciate the good things in your life.

25-29: You are really not feeling gratitude. You are having trouble seeing the good things in your life.

below 25: You are lacking gratitude. You focus on the negative aspects of your life and don't give credit for the things that are going well.

Exercise 4: Increasing Your Gratitude

The gratitude quiz can help you see how much you value the gifts in your life. Robert Emmons, a psychologist who studies the effects of expressing gratitude on well-being finds that people who regularly express their appreciation for the good things in their lives get more physical exercise, have fewer physical symptoms, and are more optimistic about their lives. According to psychologist Sonja Lyubomirsky, "The practice of gratitude is incompatible with negative emotions and may actually diminish or deter such feelings as anger, bitterness, and greed." When you feel gratitude you are expressing appreciation for the things that are good in your life now, and the people and things that made your current life good. As you've learned in earlier chapters, focusing on your life as it is now can increase your chances of finding opportunities to make your life better. Gratitude is mindfulness (intentional focus on the present moment) linked with positive emotion. When you find yourself in a present situation that is bleak and you are struggling to find something positive, you can still look forward to the best possible outcome for your situation and express advanced gratitude.

Some of the tried and true ways to increase the experience of gratitude include keeping a gratitude journal or writing a letter of thanks. Keeping a gratitude journal can be as simple as listing three things that happened during the day that you are grateful for. If you do this daily you will begin to search for good things in your life. A very powerful gratitude exercise is writing a letter of gratitude to someone you appreciate. Even better, if it is possible for you to read the letter aloud to the person, you will both experience positive emotions that have psychological benefits.

One of my former students, named Lauren, wrote me a letter of gratitude when she became a teacher herself. She thanked me for making her feel like she mattered, which made her want to do well in my class. She told me that she instills the same feelings of importance in her own students. I was particularly moved when I learned that she teaches in an extremely poor and crime-ridden school district. As she said in her letter, "ignoring the fact that students were wearing ankle bracelets and leaving class to give birth, I got to know them as people." Knowing that I helped to inspire this amazingly giving woman has meant so much to me. Her letter of gratitude is something I cherish.

Since Heather and I often include hikes or long walks on our road trips, the gratitude exercise I would recommend is a gratitude walk. Walking in nature can be a form of meditation. Meditation involves focused thought, reflection, or contemplation. Walking in nature can provide you quiet time alone with your thoughts. Walking in nature is also a chance to extend your thanks to everything that surrounds you. Walking will release endorphins that give you a boost, so you receive a health benefit in addition to the gratitude. If your mobility is limited you can do this exercise in a wheelchair. Or you can take a gratitude "walk" in your mind. Just close your eyes and imagine you are doing the following steps for a gratitude walk.

1) Choose a place to walk that is either interesting or beautiful or both. For example, you may walk in a scenic wood, or through a quaint town.

2) Make sure that you are comfortably dressed, not hungry, and not in need of a bathroom.

3) Tuck your cellphone away in a safe place so you aren't distracted.

4) As you walk in the place that you have chosen, notice the things around you. Notice the colors you see, the sounds you hear, and the smells in the air. Feel grateful for each item that draws your attention. Think about why you appreciate each thing. For example, you might appreciate the way the sun shines on the water.

5) After you have been walking for a few minutes, you will notice the physical changes that come with walking. You may feel warmer. Your bones may feel less stiff. Give thanks for your ability to take this walk. Give thanks for every part of your body that participates in this walk.

6) Finally, let your mind wander to the people and opportunities in your life that you are grateful for. Sometimes we take people and opportunities for granted. Getting some distance from those things on a gratitude walk gives us time to reflect on how much we appreciate the people and opportunities in our lives.

7) Bring the attitude of gratitude with you when you return home. Continue to appreciate the things you encounter during the day.

≈≈≈ HAUNTED HOUSES
AND HIGH TRESTLES

Heather often plans road trips with a haunted theme or a paranormal twist. Even though, she tells me she hates to be scared, Heather plans these scary excursions because she knows that I am interested in ghosts and the paranormal. She says that she likes to do scary activities with me because she knows we will laugh together and it won't be scary anymore. I feel the same way. Even though I am fascinated by things I don't understand, I don't really like being scared. I do like what happens when Heather and I find ourselves in scary situations and we help each other get through it. Some of the road trips we have taken have created moments of real fear.

Heather tried to generate fear when she planned a paranormal road trip in Northern New Jersey. On this trip, we stopped at a Paranormal Book Store in Asbury Park, New Jersey. Unfortunately, the book store was closed and we had just missed the ghost tour that had departed from the front of the book store. These near misses don't surprise us anymore. We laugh when we fail to find the thing we set out to see in the first place, and we anticipate where the adventure will lead. We like the mystery of the journey. Even though the bookstore was closed, the psychic shop two doors down was open. Heather encouraged me to get a psychic reading. Heather didn't want a reading for herself because she worries about what she will bring into her life from the other side. I told her she must believe in the paranormal more than I do if she fears spiritual repercussions from a psychic reading. I see psychic readings as entertainment, and sometimes an opportunity for synchronicity, and I feel my level of fear with the paranormal is in my control. Heather doesn't know what will happen if spirits show up. I had a sense of déjà vu when I found out we were in search of spirits in Asbury Park, New Jersey. I finally remembered that a haunted restaurant in that very town had been featured in an episode of a show I like called *Dead Files*.

On the way home from that road trip, we drove by the house that was used for the exterior shots of the house in the movie, *The Amityville Horror*. *The Amityville Horror* is based on a book about a family who moves into a house in Amityville, New York, where a mass murder had been committed the year before. The family who moves into the house has a series of paranormal experiences. Since the filmmakers were denied access to the house in New York for filming, exterior shots of the movie house were taken from a house in Toms River, New Jersey and the interior shots were filmed in a studio in California.

When we arrived at the house in Toms River around one o'clock in the morning, the house was dark and looked uninhabited. However, there were several large trash bins lined up at the end of the driveway. The trash bins all displayed the house address in sloppy red paint. It looked a lot like blood and we wouldn't have been surprised to find a body part protruding from one of the trash containers! The house address was 18 Brooks Road, and as I mentioned earlier, Brooks is a name that makes me feel a connection to things I cannot explain.

Another scary time, where the fear was manufactured, was a visit to a haunted candle shop in the Pocono Mountains of Pennsylvania. We knew the shop was supposed to be haunted so we started experiencing strange things even before we took the haunted tour. Up in the gift shop, things seemed to jump off the shelves in front of us. When we took the haunted tour in the basement of the candle shop, the tour guide spooked us with stories of the mad scientist who used to inhabit the building and the unethical experiments he conducted in the basement. According to the tour guide, the basement had housed monkeys used for unethical experiments and the spirits of these abused monkeys were now trapped in the basement of the candle shop. At one point I felt a hand tap me on the shoulder and I jumped. The tour guide laughed because she had seen Heather tap me, although Heather had moved far away by the time I turned around.

Often the fear on our road trips would arise when we got ourselves into situations we weren't sure we could get ourselves out of. For example, we wanted the horses at Assateague Island to approach our car, but when one stuck his head into Heather's car window, she was truly afraid. When we hiked in a park called the Devil's Hopyard in Connecticut, we found ourselves lost with no cell phone reception. We were afraid we might not find the trail again before the sun went down. When we checked into a scary hotel in East Stroudsburg we weren't sure we would survive the night. Fortunately, we survived all of those fearful situations. The horse moved away from the car window, we were able to locate the park trail before dusk, and we woke up alive in our hotel room.

One moment of fear that had a profound effect on us happened when we visited a park by Saint Peters Village in Pennsylvania. The hike in the park began well. It was a beautiful day and the trails seemed well marked. As we hiked, we encountered a group of hikers who climb with their remote control cars. That was interesting to see. As they navigated the trails, they used radio controls to drive their small cars over rocks and crevices. At one point, the trail we were hiking on led to a trestle bridge above a creek. The shaky open bridge was at least 30 feet above the shallow water. Heather bravely walked out onto the bridge and began to cross. I followed.

After about 20 steps, I was suddenly overcome with fear. I was sure I would plummet to my death. I froze in my tracks and I couldn't continue. I dropped to my knees and held onto the wooden beams of the track with my hands. I called out to Heather to let her know I couldn't continue. At first she laughed, not sure if I was serious. She couldn't turn around on the skinny bridge, so she stopped and turned her head. When she saw me crouched down on the bridge about 15 feet behind her, she began to feel fear too. She immediately dropped to her knees. She asked if I wanted to continue crawling across the bridge, but as I looked forward all I could think about was the great height and how I could fall if I continued. Fear had literally stopped us in our tracks. We slowly backed our way off the trestle bridge. At times we had to stop moving and just cling to the bridge because we couldn't stop laughing. Our fear seemed so irrational, yet it was powerful enough to keep us from moving forward. The experience was meaningful for us because it made us realize we are not invincible and sometimes we will meet obstacles that we cannot surmount.

About a year later, Heather sent me a link to a video of some people crossing Brave Men's Bridge, also called "Haohan Qiao." This bridge, in Shiniuzhai National Geographic Park in China, is 984 feet long and 590 feet high. Watching people cross the bridge in the video was so interesting because it looked like us in the trestle. Some people dropped to their knees and crawled. One advantage to the Brave Men's Bridge is that it has handrails. People can close their eyes and guide themselves across with the ropes. Heather and I did not have that option at Saint Peters Village.

Fear can prevent us from achieving the life we want to live. Even though we may be excited by our big dreams, they can terrify us as well. Abraham Maslow, the American Psychologist best known for creating the hierarchy of needs has said:

"We fear our highest possibilities. We are generally afraid to become that which we can glimpse in our most perfect moments, under conditions of great courage. We enjoy and even thrill to godlike possibilities we see in ourselves in such peak moments. And yet we simultaneously shiver with weakness, awe, and fear before these very same possibilities."

Are You Afraid?

Please rate the following statements based on your experience:

N = never   R = rarely   S = sometimes   O = often   A = all the time

	N	R	S	O	A
I worry that I will get sick					
I am afraid that people I love will hurt me					
I am concerned that I may lose my job or source of income					
I am frightened that I will end up alone					
I worry that I will embarrass myself					
I am afraid of failure					
I am concerned that I may end up in poverty					
I am frightened that I will die before I am ready to go					
I worry that I am not good enough to achieve my goals					
I am afraid that people will criticize me					

	N	R	S	O	A
I am concerned that my life has been meaningless					
I am frightened that I will lose control of my life					

To score this quiz :

Never=1, Rarely=2, Sometimes=3, Often=4, All the Time=5

Add up the boxes you checked to get a total score.

Now rate your level of fear:

If you scored:

above 50: You are extremely fearful. Your fear will prevent you from taking actions that could lead to a better life for you.

45-49: You are very fearful. Your fear might be preventing you from living the life you want.

40-44: You are fearful. If you try some techniques for changing your thinking and eliminating your fear you may find more enjoyment in your life.

35-39: You have an average level of fear. Your fear makes you cautious. But don't let it keep you from opportunities that could improve your life.

30-34: You are not fearful. You do not seem to experience irrational fear.

25-29: You are very unafraid. You are brave and this bravery may lead you to take risks that other people would not. Sometimes a great opportunity is worth the risk.

below 25: You are extremely unafraid. To achieve your goals you need to be realistic. Don't be so brave that you do things recklessly.

Exercise 5: Conquering Fear

The fear quiz reveals how fearful you are at this point in your life. Your fear may be preventing you from realizing your dreams. It is not surprising that many people are afraid of failure. No one wants to experience pain, loss, or humiliation. However, it may seem counterintuitive that people also fear success. Some people sabotage their own happiness because they are afraid of what will happen if they succeed. Ultimately, what we fear is change.

Fear of Failure

The fear of failure, "atychiphobia," is the fear that we will not achieve the benchmark we have set for ourselves. To determine this benchmark, we may look at the performance of people around us or use an established measure, like a score below 70% is a failure. Perfectionists are prone to a fear of failure. A fear of failure can stop us in our tracks. Some people think if you don't try, then you can't fail. But not trying is the only way to guarantee a failure.

Think of our road trip analogy. If you don't get in your car and head toward your destination, you will surely fail to reach your destination. We can use the road trip analogy to reframe how we think about failure. If you apply for a job and don't get it, you probably think you failed. However, if you are driving down the road and you come to a road block, you have also failed to reach your goal. Instead of labeling these road blocks "failure," try to see them as places where you need to change your course, not a definitive failure to reach your goal.

To reduce your fear of failure, try applying the steps below to a specific situation in your own life.

1) Analyze all potential outcomes
2) Use positive thinking
3) Look at the worst case scenario
4) Have a contingency plan

Think of something that you have been wanting to do, but have been afraid to try. You might look back at your "big dreams" exercise for an idea. Take a moment to 1) think about all of the possible outcomes if you try. To alleviate your fear of failure, 2) focus on the positive. Imagine how things could turn out right for you if you do try. When that nagging doubt creeps in, allow yourself to 3) consider the worst case scenario. Chances are good that even if the worst case scenario happens it won't be as bad as you are expecting. Now 4) create a contingency plan. What will you do if things don't turn out the way you hope they will? Having this plan in place should reduce your fear.

Fear of Success

A fear of success seems counterintuitive. Isn't success what we want to achieve? There are at least three general reasons we fear success. First, if we succeed, we may find ourselves in new situations and that can be scary. In these new situations, people will expect us to continue to succeed. For example, if I succeed at getting a promotion, I will be taking on new responsibilities. Am I prepared to handle those responsibilities?

Second, we may worry that success represents selling out (fear we are choosing personal success over integrity). I have always argued that I love being an adjunct professor because of the freedom I have. If I ever got a tenure track position that might seem like a betrayal of my earlier stance.

Finally, we may fear that success will change us in a negative way (fear of standing out, being extraordinary). Maybe we fear we will lose our modesty or sense of compassion. Maybe we will lose friends who now think we are acting superior.

Another reason we fear success is that we believe that losses will impact our lives more than gains. When confronted with a risky opportunity where we could lose $100 or win $100, we think the loss of $100 would be more harmful to us than the gain of $100 would be beneficial. To avoid loss, we avoid success. If we are not successful, we have less to lose. For example, if a person achieves his optimal health, then it seems he has nowhere to go but down.

People who fear success tend to engage in self-sabotage. They don't complete projects. They talk about what they are going to do more than they actually do it. They work on several projects but don't give any one project the attention it needs. Their self-sabotage ensures that they will not succeed.

To reduce your fear of success, try applying the steps below to a specific situation in your own life.

1) **Visualize success**. What would "success" mean for you?

2) **Decide how you will you handle success**. Will you celebrate? Set a new goal? Take that off your goal list and quit?

3) **Practice gratitude**. If you worry that others will resent you for your success, then don't focus on your bragging rights. Imagine all the people you can thank for their assistance with your success.

Take a moment to consider something that you have avoided because you are afraid that you will succeed. For example, maybe you believe you have a lot to contribute to local politics, but you don't run for office. Your failure to run for office may not be a worry that you will humiliate yourself, but a fear about what will happen if you are the new town mayor. Think through the possible outcomes.

What if you *do* run for office and you are successful? Can you think of the positive things you can achieve in that position instead of focusing on the resentment from others and increased responsibility? What is the first thing you would do when you learned you were the new town Mayor? Who would you thank and who would you want around you as you made your acceptance speech?

Fear of Change

Most people resist change. Doing something new and different can be scary. If the old thing we are doing isn't terrible, it is very hard to find the momentum to do something new. That is why we are often more motivated by "the stick" than "the carrot." If you want to get a horse to move, you could offer a reward (carrot) or punish the horse until he moves (whack him with a stick). When I talk to my friends about their potential job changes I often hear that they have been offered great benefits (carrot) if they change jobs, but they resist due to the uncertainty involved with the career change. My friends who are finally willing to make the move to a new job are friends who find themselves in working environments that are just too bad to stay (stick).

We fear change most when we feel out of control. When Viktor Frankl was in a concentration camp, where all control was stripped away from him, he learned the importance of freedom and control. Frankl found that a shift in his perspective could return his sense of control. In the concentration camp he learned to look for the things he *could* control rather than focusing on the things he could not control. For example, he could still control his thoughts and his responses to various situations, even when he could not control the situations themselves.

To reduce your fear of change, try applying the steps below to a specific situation in your own life.

1) Understand your freedom to choose
2) Reframe the situation when you cannot change it
3) Seek support

Consider an upcoming change in your life. First consider your role in this change. Change can be scary when it makes us feel powerless, but you can remind yourself that you probably had an active role in moving toward this change. If you feel that you truly have no control over the change that has happened or is about to happen, then you should reframe the situation in an optimistic light. Instead of focusing on the loss, ask yourself what will be gained when this change occurs. Even the worst of circumstances tend to produce some positive change. Finally, find people who can help you through the transition. Share your feelings with people you trust and people who can relate to the change you are experiencing. You may even be able to find a support group designed specifically for people who are going through the change you fear.

≈≈≈ BACKING OUT
OF A CRANBERRY BOG

Heather and I learned from our experience on the high trestle at Saint Peters Village that sometimes we cannot proceed as planned. The fear that we might plummet to our deaths stopped us in our tracks. Looking forward, we desperately wanted to reach the end of the trestle, but we just couldn't proceed. Once you get set on a course it is hard to imagine that things could be any different. But when you cannot go forward, you must find a way to go back.

One November, Heather picked me up and we headed toward a destination she would not disclose. She only told me that it might involve some off-road driving. As we drove through the Pine Barrens in New Jersey, she made a turn into Whitesbog Village, a historical village founded by the Whitesbog family in the early 1900's. Although Whitesbog was established as a cranberry bog, Elizabeth White found a way to grow blueberries on the land as well.

The White family did not live in Whitesbog Village, but 41 cranberry workers lived in homes at Whitesbog with their families.

When the village was active it included a general store, a post office, a schoolhouse, a water tower, and cranberry-processing buildings. Many of these buildings still stand today. When Heather and I visited, we went into the Whitesbog General Store and purchased some delicious Cranberry Bog Frogs, made of chocolate and cranberries. Then we headed out for a driving tour of the cranberry bogs.

Maps were provided at the general store and Heather also found a comprehensive guide to the village and bog on-line. The online guide described all the flora and fauna we might see as we made our way through the bogs. As I read aloud from the online guide, "Frogs are fond of this borrow pit, so you'll very likely hear them croaking here. Listen for the leopard frog, which croaks a deep, rhythmic, rattling snore..." we began to hear the snoring sound of frogs right on cue!

Driving through the cranberry bog, we found ourselves on skinny sand roads surrounded by water-filled cranberry bogs. One turn in the wrong direction and the car would be sunk in the bog, or stuck in the mud. The map we had gotten from the general store showed a pond called Otter Pond on the other side of the bog. We decided to head in that direction in search of otters. Unfortunately, the map showed an impassible road on the way to Otter Pond. Heather was undeterred by the map and said we should keep going that direction anyway. As it turned out, the map was correct. When we got to that spot, the road was impassible. The skinny sand road led up to a drop off into an area of deep water that stretched about 20 feet before the sand road resumed. Once we reached the drop off we couldn't turn around and go back because the sandy path we were on was a narrow road surrounded by bog on either side. The only solution was to drive the car backward and exit in the same way we had entered.

Heather panicked and said she could not back the car out without driving us into the bog. Since I have a very long driveway and I often have to back all the way out (especially when I have only shoveled a small path through the snow), I volunteered to back out the car. Within the car we climbed over each other to change places; the path was not wide enough for us to get out of the car and walk around. As I started moving the car backward we heard loud engine noises. It sounded like a vehicle was approaching us at a high rate of speed. Heather and I exchanged looks of panic. We couldn't move if something fast was coming up behind us! Heather remembered there was an air strip nearby and we agreed that it might be a small plane running parallel to the road we were on. As I started to back up, two motorcycles rushed up behind us. Their engines were the sound we had heard. When they saw us blocking the road, they were able to stop and navigate back to wherever they had come from. If we had not been blocking the path, they may have sped right into the ditch filled with water.

Driving backward was scary, but it was the only way out. And it was also empowering. Backing out of that cranberry bog felt like a life lesson, even at the moment it was happening. Life throws water-filled ditches at us sometimes and when that happens it may be impossible to keep moving forward on the current path.

At these moments we need to know it is okay to move backward, to get to a place where it is safe enough to move forward in a different direction. For example, a dead end job with no possibility of making it more fulfilling, or an unhappy marriage, may stop you in your tracks. The solution may be to admit it was the wrong path for you and back yourself out of it. Like the cranberry bog, getting back out may be much harder than getting in. But there is no other choice unless you want to get stuck or sink. The bad choice you made to take that road may leave you with good stories like the story of our escape from the cranberry bog. Take your stories and get off that path; don't keep going forward on that road!

In the fear chapter I described an experience that Heather and I had on a high trestle in Saint Peters Village. When the fear became overwhelming, we knew we could not go forward. It was scary to crawl backwards along the trestle that we had been eager to walk across moments before. But we laughed at ourselves and it was fun to be scared because we knew even though it wouldn't be an easy trip back, it was a safer journey and we would be okay. We probably looked ridiculous crawling backwards, but sometimes it's okay to choose the path that will give you the best possible outcome, even if changing your course makes you feel foolish. Think of the courage it takes for a middle aged woman to go back to school and begin the journey to a new career. As Heather and I have learned on our road trips, being willing to change your course is crucial to finding your best possible outcome.

Are You Willing to Change Your Course of Action?

Please rate the following statements based on your experience: SD = Strongly Disagree D = Disagree A = Agree SA = Strongly Agree					
	SD	D	Not Sure	A	SA
I am open to advice about how to invest my money					
I would be willing to start a new career tomorrow					
I would change my residence to advance my life goals					
I am willing to end a relationship if it brings me more pain than joy					
I would consider going back to school if I need to train for a new career					
I am open to advice about establishing new patterns of interaction with my family					
I would give up the possessions I have acquired to finance my dreams					
I am willing to explore other religions					

	SD	D	Not Sure	A	SA
I would change my political affiliation if another party was more aligned with my needs					
I would apologize and correct my mistake if I learned I was wrong					
I would change my "yes" to a "no" if I realized I had committed to more than I felt comfortable doing					
When I realize I am lost, I stop and go back to a point where I was not lost					

To score this quiz :

SD =1, D =2, Not Sure =3, A =4, SA =5

Add up the boxes you checked to get a total score.

Now rate your level of flexibility:

If you scored:

above 50: You are extremely adaptable. This means you are easily able to reverse your course if you are not on the right track to your goal.

45-49: You are very adaptable. This means you are able to switch your course when necessary.

40-44: You are adaptable. This means you can figure out how to change your course.

35-39: You have an average level of adaptability. You may need an outside nudge to switch your course.

30-34: You are inflexible. It would take a big push for you to change your course.

25-29: You are very inflexible. You are resistant to change. Once you set a course of action you want to stick with it.

below 25: You are extremely inflexible. You are highly resistant to change.

Exercise 6: Where You Could Change Your Course

When you are young it is easier to turn around because you have covered less distance on your journey. You may be less committed to a particular course. As we age, people explore the world and make decisions about what they believe and where they want their lives to go. Psychologists have come up with four categories of people based on how they decided on a belief or course of action, how they created their identity.

A psychologist named James Marcia studied identity formation in young adults and found there are two things that influence how we select an identity:

1) An exploration of possible options
2) A commitment to one of the options

Using these components, Marcia created four distinct identity statuses:

Identity Achievement (commitment follows exploration)
Identity Foreclosure (commitment without exploration)
Identity Moratorium (exploration without commitment)
Identity Diffusion (a lack of exploration or commitment)

People classified as "Achieved" are people who have explored many options and committed to a selected course.

For example, you may decide to be a banker after trying several careers and realizing banking is the best fit for you.

People who are in "Foreclosure" have not explored their options, but they have committed to a path. This would be true if you decided to be a banker because your dad was a banker and you never considered doing anything else.

People in "Moratorium" are continuing to explore their options, but have not committed to any course of action. If you are still exploring your career options, but have not committed to one, you are in moratorium. For young adults, it is healthy to spend some time in moratorium, but life may become stressful if you continue to stay in this state as you age.

Finally, people who are in "Diffusion" have not explored their options and have not committed to a path. This would be the case if you have no idea what career you want to pursue and you haven't even given it much thought. A life in diffusion can be very stressful and also damaging to your self-esteem.

To go back to our road trip analogy, when you are "Achieved" you have considered all of the possible routes you could take and selected the best one for your journey. If you are in "Foreclosure" you have chosen to follow the routes someone suggested without considering other options. If you are in "Moratorium" you may be considering many options This state may lead you to drive around for a while and try new paths. This course may be good for enhancing synchronicities if you are mindful as you explore your options. Ideally, you reach a point where you commit to a route to reach your destination. If you are in "Diffusion" you don't know how to get to your destination and you haven't explored any options for how to get there. Chances are good that your road trip will never materialize.

A state of exploration is necessary before you can settle into the best course for you. People who are foreclosed will have a hard time when they hit a road block because they aren't aware of any other routes to their goal. The following exercise will help you explore some options as you think about the course of your life.

1) Consider your **career path**. Ask yourself:
   Where am I on my career path?
   Where will I end up if I stay on this course?
   Is that where I want to be?
   If yes, then stay the course.
   If no, where do you want to be?
   Take a minute to think about a different path to get where you want to go.
   Is there anything you need to let go of or undo to get on the right path?

2) Consider your **romantic life**. Ask yourself:
   Where am I in my relationship?
   Where will I end up if I stay on this course?
   Is that where I want to be?
   If yes, then stay the course.

If no, where do you want to be?

Take a minute to think about a different path to get where you want to go.

Is there anything you need to let go of or undo to get on the right path?

3) Consider your **spirituality**. Ask yourself:

Where am I in my spiritual journey?

Where will I end up if I stay on this course?

Is that where I want to be?

If yes, then stay the course.

If no, where do you want to be?

Take a minute to think about a different path to get where you want to go.

Is there anything you need to let go of or undo to get on the right path?

4) Consider your **physical health**. Ask yourself:

What are my current health habits?

Where will I end up if I stay on this course?

Is that where I want to be?

If yes, then stay the course.

If no, where do you want to be?

Take a minute to think about a different path to get where you want to go.

Is there anything you need to let go of or undo to get on the right path?

Repeat this exercise for any other life goals you have.

≈≈≈ NO HORSES, GHOSTS, OR TINY CHURCHES

Over many road trips, Heather and I have noticed that we often fail to find the physical item or destination we set out to find. When we went to Chincoteague, an island in Virginia that is inhabited by wild horses, we found the beach, but no horses. We were able to get back on the road and drive to Assateague, another island near Chincoteague, where we did find some horses. When we took a ghost tour in West Chester, Pennsylvania we were disappointed that no ghosts appeared. After every spooky story the tour guide would say, "And so it turned out it was not a ghost." There was always some logical explanation for the phenomenon people had experienced at that location. No ghosts on the ghost tour? We also failed to find the tiny church we were searching for in New Jersey. Although we searched up and down the road using the address we had for the Tiny Church, it never materialized.

Over many trips, we have learned when we fail to find the things we are looking for it makes our road trips even more meaningful. We realize the trip is about so much more than the destination. The trip is about personal growth. Often personal growth comes about as a result of our interactions with others. As we fail to find the physical things we are looking for, it creates a shared experience, a connecting bond. The fact that we can laugh about our failure to find ghosts and horses gives us a unique bond. These trips together have given us a safe space to work through disappointments and help us to understand each other better.

One night in June, Heather asked me drive us to the Alison pest control company in New Jersey. She would not reveal what she expected to find. We drove into the pest control parking lot at night in the dark. The business had been closed for hours and I was worried that someone would report our presence on the property. Heather seemed very disappointed that the oddity she was searching for did not seem to be there. She bravely walked across the lawn near the Alison Pest Control sign and found the cement base that once held the oddity we had come to see. Shaking her head, she finally told me that we had driven to Wall, New Jersey to see a giant ant! The giant ant, measuring at least 10 feet, had been created to attract business to the pest control company. When I learned what we were searching for, I was actually relieved that the giant ant had disappeared!

We wondered where the giant ant had gone and

speculated the pest control business might take it inside at night. After the trip, we searched for the ant on the internet and learned that the township had asked the pest control company to remove it because it violated their definition of a business sign. Even before we knew the giant ant was a sign, we had wondered if the missing ant could be a "sign" of something in our lives. Since we had both recently spotted ants trying to invade our homes, we hoped it was a sign that the summer ants would soon disappear.

For Heather and me, the state of Maine is a place of personal connection. Our father grew up in Maine and Heather and I traveled there every year to see our relatives. We feel a warm connection to certain places in Maine. Our relatives live in Old Town, Maine, the original home of the Old Town Canoe. Our paternal grandfather, who we affectionately called "Grampy Joe," would take us out on the Penobscot River in his aluminum canoe.

Another treasured landmark for is LaBree's Bakery. The LaBree's factory in Old Town, Maine makes and ships delicious donuts and other baked goods. Attached to the factory is a donut thrift shop where visitors can purchase the delicious treats on site. Our favorite items from the bakery are the chocolate cake donuts with sugar and the chocolate cake donuts with coconut. There are no donuts like these cake donuts in Pennsylvania. Whenever we take a trip to Maine we have to return with LaBree's donuts to share with any family members that couldn't make the trip.

When we went in search of covered bridges in Berks County, Pennsylvania, Heather was discouraged that we failed to find some of the bridges on her list. As we sat in a parking lot reviewing our plans, we realized we were not far from our brother's place of employment in Shillington, Pennsylvania. We decided to stop by unannounced and visit our brother Joe at work. He seemed very happy to see us and it was great to see him busy at work in a job he enjoys. Since he lives an hour away from me now, I don't see him very often. When I do see him, it is because he makes the trip down to see my family, so it was nice that Heather and I could show up in his town and surprise him there.

On our trip to Asbury Park, New Jersey, Heather made a connection with a psychic medium. The psychic was trying to read my tarot cards, but she was distracted by Heather. She was sure she knew Heather from somewhere. Heather did not recognize the psychic so they concluded that Heather must have a familiar-looking face. That sense of familiarity, like a synchronicity, can make you pause and pay attention to the moment. The personal connection to that psychic prompted Heather to remember previous encounters with boardwalk psychics. She told me that the most accurate psychic reading she ever received came from a boardwalk psychic.

While Heather looks for oddities on our road trips, I often use these trips to explore the elusive connections I have with people who have been in my life. One road trip took us to the grave of my college boyfriend. As we drove, Heather allowed me to revisit that relationship and think about how I approach romantic relationships in general.

When we visited the psychic, she made a connection with another close friend of mine who had recently died. Again, this gave me a chance to think about that relationship as we drove. Driving through East Stroudsburg in the Poconos, and failing to find Rural Route 4, allowed me some time to process my relationship with the man who lived on the elusive road.

One autumn day, Heather and I drove to a town called Bangor, Pennsylvania because we have a connection to a place in Maine with the same name. We did find some similarities between the towns. Both towns seem to reflect a simpler way of life, small towns with friendly people. I grew up visiting Bangor in Maine and didn't even know there was one in Pennsylvania until Heather took me there. It was interesting to learn that people in Pennsylvania call their town "Banger."

I remember our stop at the Pink Cadillac Diner in Natural Bridge, Virginia as a destination that strengthened my personal connections. That is the first time that I actually remember Heather telling me that she does not like to eat ice cream. This may seem like a small thing, but when I think about how many of our road trips include a stop for ice cream, I realize how hard Heather works to make sure the people in her life are happy. As we took pictures at this diner, we were sending them to a man I had just met, but would end up dating for almost a year. Again, Heather was nurturing a growing relationship.

The best thing about the connection that Heather and I share through our road trips is the hysterical laughter.

I will never forget the morning we watched elderly women doing chair aerobics on a morning workout show when we woke up in a hotel in Virginia. We pulled up some chairs and joined in. Sometimes our laughter comes from the joy we experience on our trips and sometimes the laughter is a release of the anxiety we feel when we find ourselves lost or in a situation we did not anticipate. Laughter truly is the best medicine.

Telling other people about our road trips also enhances our personal connections. When a friend of mine whom I call "Bob the Lawyer" posted on Facebook that he was taking his kids to Brooklyn and asked for activity suggestions, I took a page out of Heather's book and google "oddities in Brooklyn, New York." I was able to send Bob a link to "Large Hat on a Pole." I hope he had some great adventures looking for that!

Are You Making the Most of Your Personal Relationships?

Please rate the following statements based on your experience: N = never R = rarely S = sometimes O = often A = all the time					
	N	R	S	O	A
I consult my friends before making a big life decision					
I answer my emails promptly					
I reach out to friends I have not heard from in a while					
I go out of my way to meet new people					
I let people know when I am thinking of them					
I create events that bring people together					
I answer my texts promptly					
I surround myself with people who share my interests					
I ask for help when I need it					
I answer my phone when it rings/buzzes					

	N	R	S	O	A
I avoid people who don't support my dreams					
I spend quality time with the people I care about					

<u>To score this quiz</u> :

Never=1, Rarely=2, Sometimes=3, Often=4, All the Time=5

Add up the boxes you checked to get a total score.

Now rate your experience with personal relationships:

If you scored:

above 50: You are extremely connected. You recognize that certain people are important to your journey and you know how to make the most of these connections.

45-49: You are very connected. You surround yourself with people who increase the quality of your life.

40-44: You are connected. You know where to find support when you need it.

35-39: You have an average level of human connection in your life. You have people you can rely on when you need them although you may not always make the most of potential connections.

30-34: You are disconnected. You want to connect with people but you have not learned to reach out to the people you need.

25-29: You are very disconnected. You don't make the most of your human connections.

below 25: You are extremely disconnected. You are not aware of the importance of human connection. You need to realize that your life could be improved if you increase your interactions with others.

Exercise 7: Developing Personal Relationships

After taking the personal relationships quiz you have a good idea of how well connected you are to the people around you. Connecting with other people is very important to living your best possible life. In the chapter about finding your passion, I introduced you to Randy Pausch. As Professor Pausch gave his last lecture, he reminded the audience that "People are the most important thing." Shawn Achor says instead of worrying about whether our glass is half empty or half full, we should be making sure we are surrounded by people who can refill it when that is necessary.

How we connect with others has a lot to do with the feedback we received as children. If we had nurturing caregivers, we will expect people to be kind to us and we will act in ways that encourage kindness. However, if our caregivers were indifferent or critical, we may act in ways that elicit that treatment from others. Our personality traits also play a role in how we connect with others. Extroverts like to meet new people, while introverts prefer less social interaction. Shy people often have trouble making personal connections because their detached demeanor makes them seem unapproachable. Narcissists have shallow human connections because they fail to respond to negative feedback. To avoid conflict, people tend to tell narcissists what they want to hear, even if it is not true.

Knowing that everyone has had different experiences with personal relationships may be the first step to improving our connections with others. In a video promoting his book *How to Succeed With People*, Paul McGee holds up a beach ball with six colored sections and spins it around to demonstrate how people can be looking at the same thing and see it completely differently. In a Positive Psychology class I taught, students described times when they had failed to take another person's perspective into account. One student related a story of how mad she was when a bus failed to arrive on time. In class she considered that there were probably extenuating circumstances that delayed the driver. She was angry at the bus driver and the bus driver was angry too, but they were looking at two different sides of the beach ball. When the student took a moment to view the world through the eyes of the bus driver, her anger diminished. We can all use perspective-taking techniques to improve our relationships with others.

Paul McGee gives four suggestions for improving your connections with others. When you interact with someone:

1) Consider what is going on in that person's life at the moment.

2) Find out what the person needs right now. Do they need your support? Encouragement? Some space?

3) Try to listen to understand, not to defend. Leave a gap in the conversation where you just listen.

4) Clearly communicate your perspective. Don't assume that the other person sees the world as you do.

Although these tips may seem obvious, it is very easy to get tied to our own perspective and to spend our energy defending our own viewpoint. We are so focused on our immediate situation that we may fail to consider where the other person is coming from (often literally). We assume we know what they need or we fail to consider their needs at all. We may be so busy defending our position that we don't even stop to hear their perspective. And finally, we assume they see the world as we do, and we shouldn't make that assumption. We need to find a way to connect with people so the beach ball can spin, allowing us to consider multiple perspectives.

Think of a person you have trouble connecting with: either you argue frequently or you just don't know the person very well. Schedule a time to talk with this person and try all of the strategies mentioned above. How did your interaction change when you took the time to clearly envision the other person's perspective and calmly communicate your own?

According to the longest happiness study ever conducted, the best predictor of lifelong happiness and well-being is personal relationships. As it turns out, the *number* of friendships we have is not important, it is the *quality* of those relationships that matters. People who have others in their life that they can trust tend to be happier, healthier, and more successful. Being able to trust someone involves two components, *intent* and *competence*. You need to surround yourself with people who want to help you (intent) and people who actually have the means to help you (competence). You may find that you have family members who truly want to help you, but don't have the means to help you. Although you love them, without competence, it will be hard to count on their support. Throughout your life you will need different types of support, so you may need to rely on many people for financial and/or emotional support. Having these people in your life will help you to live the best possible life you can envision for yourself. As Barbara Streisand sings, "People who need people are the luckiest people in the world."

As you work to expand and enhance your personal connections try the following:

1) **Be genuine**. Personal connections are based on understanding, so you need to reveal your true self.

2) **Offer help**. A great way to increase your personal connections is to offer assistance to others. Remember to find out what they need. Don't assume you know what type of help is needed.

3) **Pay attention and really listen**. To create a true connection you need to see their perspective.

4) **Be vulnerable**. Sometimes you will need help and you need to feel comfortable reaching out to your connections for help.

One assignment in my Positive Psychology class required students to complete ten acts of kindness throughout the semester. Students messaged me to tell me what they had done and the consequences of their actions. I decided at the beginning of the semester that any act the student submitted would earn a point. Acts of kindness ranged from holding a door for the next person coming through to offering a homeless person shelter and a meal. The biggest reward the students got from completing these acts of kindness was an increase in their personal connections. Many students met neighbors and classmates they never would have spoken to if they hadn't been looking for ways to reach out to others.

Students also learned about taking the other person's perspective. Some students were disappointed when their help was refused or people seemed ungrateful. Students learned that they needed to ask questions to find out what kind of help would be appreciated before they jumped in to save the day. For example, when one student saw a neighbor rush into their house in a hurry leaving the car door open, the student "helped" by shutting the car door. Minutes later, when the neighbor came out with his arms full of things he wanted to put into the car, he was not happy to find the door closed. Always make sure you know what kind of assistance would be helpful.

≈≈≈ AND THEN THERE WERE LLAMAS

One January, Heather and I took a spontaneous road trip to shake the winter blahs. She warned me as we headed out that she had planned a trip including many destinations best seen during the summer, but that we would make the best of it. She didn't tell me any specifics about where we were headed.

The day started with a trip to the Daniel Boone Homestead in Birdsboro, Pennsylvania. This historic site was the childhood home of American frontiersman Daniel Boone. His original log home no longer stands, but you can tour the stone home that stands on the original foundation. During the spring, summer and fall there are many things to see at the homestead. In addition to the home you can tour a barn, a blacksmith shop, a bake house and a smokehouse that were added after the Boones moved off the property. You will find a picnic grove, a lake, and trails for hikers and equestrians.

When we went there in January, many of the trails were snow covered, but Heather and I found areas to explore. We trekked across the snow to take pictures by a waterfall and the old saw mill. We stopped to have a conversation with a Boy Scout leader whose troop had spent the night in a camping lodge on the homestead. He described the trails we weren't able to access and encouraged us to bring our horses on our next visit. Maybe we will return again when the weather is nicer, but seeing the homestead in an off season is more typical of the types of road trip adventures Heather and I have.

Our next stop was a vineyard where we purchased some wine and appreciated the venue. In warmer months it would be a lovely place to have lunch and sip wine outside, but since it was winter, we got back into the car right after we made our purchases. As we headed toward our third stop, Heather said, "I have the address, but I can't remember where we are going or why!" As we approached the address, it turned out to be an ice cream shop. It seemed early in the day for ice cream and this also would have been a better treat on a summer day. However, as we pulled in Heather added, "And they also have a petting zoo!"

We were at the Oley Turnpike Dairy. Our road trips often include stops at an ice cream shop, but this time we didn't eat any ice cream. Instead, we headed straight back to the petting zoo. We passed many goats and then we heard some strange sounds coming from one of the enclosures. As we made our way around the corner, we found a pair of mating llamas! If you have never heard mating llamas, they make a sound called an "orgle." It is kind of a gargling sound. The llama, native to South America, is a relative of the camel, but the llama does not have a hump. I don't see llamas very often so I was surprised to learn that it isn't too hard to find llamas in my home state of Pennsylvania. There are several llama farms throughout the state. Coming upon those mating llamas created an awkward moment. I'm sure the llamas didn't care who passed by, but we quietly walked down another path.

As we came to the end of the petting zoo, we met a family that had come to take care of a sick monkey that was housed in a facility not accessible to the public. After we talked to the family, I learned that Heather doesn't like monkeys very much. I do like monkeys, although I have never been close enough to interact with one. Heather and I don't like all of the same things. We don't agree on everything. What we have is a shared appreciation for the journey and an understanding of the give and take nature of a relationship. She often says, "You're such a good sport!" when we get off course or when things don't go as planned, but she has no idea how much I appreciate her taking the time to plan these trips, and the weekends she gives up to go on these adventures with me. Through these interactions with Heather, I have learned to take the time to listen to people and appreciate different points of view.

Whenever Heather and I talk about people we have met on our road trips, we recount the story of the homeless man we met in in a church. On a road trip to Philadelphia, Heather and I attended a comedy show. The show was in a building that also housed church services. We arrived early for the show so we waited in the lobby. As we were waiting, a disheveled man came into the building and approached us.

"I've missed the last bus to the suburbs," he said. "My mother is sick and I need to get to her. Can you give me some money so I can take a taxi?"

His story made me tear up and I gave him a hug. I immediately opened my wallet and asked how much he needed. He told me, accepted the money, and went on his way. Heather later confessed that she was shocked that I had pulled out my wallet in front of a stranger. Asking for money for a taxi could have been a ruse to get drug money. We both agreed that a church was probably a good place to go when you are in need. As we listened to his story, we were also listening to our intuition as well, and we each had different reactions to the situation.

It was hard to hear the psychic medium in Asbury Park, New Jersey because there were so many distractions around. As the psychic read my tarot cards, her baby son was whimpering in a stroller by her side. The shop door was open, allowing all the sounds of the busy street to enter. In the middle of the reading, the psychic's daughter came in; the psychic paused several times to admonish the daughter for touching all of the tarot cards. At the end of the reading, the psychic told me not to share what I heard during my reading because it would bring bad karma. I have had many psychic readings and no one has ever told me that a reading is confidential. I did an internet search and I couldn't find any warnings about sharing what a psychic predicts.

The psychic said I could talk to Heather about the reading because she was present during the reading. At one point, the psychic said, "If the baby gets fussy, just push the stroller." Heather jumped up to care for the baby and the psychic laughed. We hadn't noticed that a man had entered the room and stood behind Heather. He was the baby's father and the psychic asked him to take the baby outside.

The psychic told me that my middle daughter would be "good with her hands." Since she was describing possible careers for my children, I assumed that meant a career with her hands. After the reading, Heather said, "It is strange that she thinks your teenage daughter who just got diagnosed with rheumatoid arthritis in her hands will want a career working with her hands. Maybe she heard the spirits wrong and she meant to tell you: *Don't worry, everything will be good with her hands.*"

Heather likes to pay for everything, so it is often a battle to see who can get the check or who will jump out to fill the gas tank. One time, as I was getting ready to pump the gas, Heather offered me her Giant gas card. I didn't want her to pay for the gas, so I said "no" and told her I would put it on my card. Before I could turn on the pump, Heather asked me to stop and listen to her. Her Giant card provides a discount of 30¢ per gallon of gas. She explained that I could still pay for the gas but I should accept her discount. That made a lot of sense and I was glad that she made me slow down and listen.

On a trip to Marsh Creek in Downingtown, Pennsylvania, Heather and I talked about relationships and finances. It was one of the most honest conversations we ever had. I felt like I learned a lot about my sister that day. Heather is so focused on others that she rarely shares details about her own life. On this walk through the park she talked a lot about her finances and life goals. She listened while I shared my ideas about a book I wanted to write. On a future trip, she opened up about her romantic history, something I had never heard anything about before. Slowly, over the course of many road trips, I am learning about the complex and amazing person she is.

When you listen to people you may learn things that are important, but sometimes people are just entertaining. At Marge's Diner in New Jersey, where Heather and I had breakfast on my birthday in 2016, the waitress was wearing a t-shirt that said, "Eat Food. Get Gas. Marge's Diner." Since it was my first time eating at this diner and I hadn't seen any gas pumps when we pulled in, I said, "Oh, I didn't know there was a gas station here." The waitress laughed and said, "There isn't a gas station here anymore. Now it's just funny."

Are You a Good Listener?

Please rate the following statements based on your experience: N = never R = rarely S = sometimes O = often A = all the time					
	N	R	S	O	A
I encourage people to talk to me					
I let people speak and do not interrupt them when they are talking					
I ask follow up questions if I am not sure I understand					
I show interest by maintaining eye contact or nodding to show I understand					
I can ignore word choice and speech patterns and focus on the message					
I ask follow up questions to encourage continued conversation					
I resist the urge to finish a sentence even if I think I know what the person will say					

	N	R	S	O	A
I can assess a person's mental state (happy, sad, frustrated, etc.) from the things he or she says					
At the end of a conversation I could summarize what was said					
I process what the person is saying so I can provide a thoughtful response					
I allow the person to completely answer one question before I ask another					
People say, "Thanks for listening."					

To score this quiz :

Never=1, Rarely=2, Sometimes=3, Often=4, All the Time=5

Add up the boxes you checked to get a total score.

Now rate your ability to listen:

If you scored:

above 50: You are an extremely good listener. You take the time to understand what another person needs or wants to communicate. You can use this skill to help others and learn valuable information.

45-49: You are a very good listener. You know that hearing the message is important.

40-44: You are a good listener. You pay attention when someone speaks to you.

35-39: Your listening skills are average. You try to pay attention and understand the message. You could improve.

30-34: You are not a good listener. You may be missing important information.

25-29: You have very poor listening skills. You need to find a way to screen out distractions and focus on the person you are listening to.

below 25: You have extremely poor listening skills. This may lead to social isolation for you. People need to know that you are paying attention and that you value what they have to say.

Exercise 8: Learning to Listen

After taking the listening quiz you have a good idea of how well you listen when others are talking. I think I am a good listener, but I have at least one friend who would say that I ask too many questions without waiting for a response. I could definitely work on that. If you also need to work on your listening skills, the following exercise could help.

Listening to people is a good way to connect with them. People like to talk about things that interest them, and people appreciate it when someone actively listens. Active listening means that the listener is hearing more than the words – the listener is connecting to the message and also understanding the emotional state of the speaker.

When you actively listen to people you can establish trust. This will help to build your human connections. Acknowledging that you've heard what they have said may be taken as a sign that you agree with what they are saying. You can use body language to show you disagree, or just listen and disagree when it is your turn to speak.

Listening can also help to increase synchronicity in your life. If you are actively listening, you may hear about an opportunity you have been waiting for. If you are in the market for a car and you let people know this, you may hear someone mention that they have a wonderful car they need to sell.

Before you do the following exercise, think about your communication style. Are you an introvert or extrovert? If you are introverted you may have fewer opportunities to practice your conversational skills. The good news is you don't have to talk to lots of people, or even dominate the conversation, to become a good listener. Think about whether you are patient or impatient. If you are impatient, you may need to work on this before you can be a good listener. Being a good listener requires that you take the time to listen to what someone else is saying. You cannot interrupt or rush them along if you want to get the full benefit of what they have to share.

Listening Exercise: Talk to someone about "big dreams."

Ask someone: "How do you know when you have found your purpose in life?"

Then use the following instructions to really hear the message the other person gives you.

1) **Be patient** (give the speaker a moment to collect his/her thoughts)

2) **Pay attention** (look at the speaker, ignore distractions and focus only on the speaker, do not think about your reply, observe their body language)

3) **Show that you are listening** (nod, smile, lean in, say "yes" and "uh-huh")

4) **Provide Feedback** (summarize what you heard, ask clarification questions)

5) **Defer Judgment** (don't interrupt, don't correct, wait until the end for your response)

6) **Respond Appropriately** (be honest with your response, assert your opinions respectfully, treat person as you want to be treated).

When I was teaching a Positive Psychology class at West Chester University in Pennsylvania, I had an opportunity to try this listening exercise with a group of 75 students. We broke into pairs and took turns asking each other "How do you know when you have found your purpose in life?"

Because there were an odd number of students, I was able to participate as well. My partner, a girl named Carly, asked me, "How do you know when you have found your purpose in life?" and listened attentively as I explained that I think I am on track to find my purpose when I enjoy what I am doing and it "feels right." Carly didn't interrupt and asked appropriate questions. Then it was my turn to listen. I thought that I would be politely nodding my head as she proceeded to say almost the same things that I had stated a moment before. But I was wrong.

According to Carly, you know you have found your purpose when the feedback from others around you is positive. Based on her answer, finding your purpose has very little to do with your own intuition and more to do with external cues. I found this exercise to be more powerful than I had imagined. Not only did I come away with some new ideas about finding your purpose, but it reinforced the fact that not everyone views the world in the same way. It is incredibly important to learn how to listen to others to see their perspective, instead of assuming we all see the world in the same way.

≈≈≈ NOT WORTH THE PRICE
OF ADMISSION

Although many of the oddities Heather and I found on our road trips could be viewed at no cost, there were others that had steep admission fees. On several occasions, we would drive to a tourist attraction and realize we didn't want to pay the fee. When that happened, we found opportunities to take fun pictures at the attraction without going inside.

One of these places was Shenandoah Caverns in Virginia. According to the brochure you can "Explore an underground world of breathtaking natural wonders, incredible geology and extraordinary crystalline formations on a one hour guided tour." I'm sure the underground caverns are phenomenal, but Heather and I decided we didn't want to spend the money required to enter the caverns. Instead, we explored the beautiful gift shop, which included a dramatic gated staircase descending into the caverns. Then we explored the property around the caverns. We found brightly colored statues and live goats to pose with for our road trip photos. I feel like I can say I have been to Shenandoah Caverns in Virginia, and one day I may want to return to see the inside of the cavern. For this trip, our adventure on the grounds provided enough adventure to justify the trip.

For one of our adventures, Heather planned a trip to a Tiki Bar on a New Jersey beach two hours from our home. When we arrived around 10 o'clock at night, we found a long line of young adults waiting to get inside and learned that entrance to the bar required a cover charge. The bar appeared to be very crowded. Since our goal was to have a quiet drink by the beach, and not be in a loud crowd, we decided to skip the Tiki Bar – the attraction that brought us to that beach in the first place! We walked on the beach by the bar and took pictures of the décor from the outside. We could hear the music playing in the bar, along with the crashing waves of the ocean. After some time with our toes in the sand, we headed back to the boardwalk and found a quieter bar with no admission fee.

Another place where we decided to skip the admission cost was Natural Bridge Park in Virginia. The town was named after a geological formation that was created by a river that carved a bridge through a mountain of limestone. The arch of the bridge is 215 feet high and the opening of the bridge spans 90 feet. This bridge cannot be seen from the roadside and you must pay an admission fee to hike the trail that leads to the bridge. Heather and I hiked along the trail until we reached the point where payment was required. Then we retreated to the air conditioned gift shop where we were able to see beautiful pictures of the Natural Bridge and read about its history.

Heather and I also found oddities that provided great photo opportunities surrounding the Natural Bridge Park. One of these oddities was a Haunted Monster Museum. Although the haunted woods and monster museum were closed for the season at the time of our visit, we were able to take pictures with the ceramic ghosts guarding the gates. Across from the Natural Bridge gift shop we found a wax museum. This museum was also closed for the season, but we snapped a photo with a wax figure who was climbing a rope on the porch by the entrance. Heather pretended to be ready to catch him if he dropped. I would love to go back and tour the haunted woods and wax museum. Unfortunately, the wax museum has permanently closed, its exhibits moved elsewhere. The building is now used for a visitor center. The haunted woods were destroyed in a fire. Sometimes when we travel too fast, we miss opportunities.

On a road trip that took us through Ocean City Maryland, we definitely traveled too fast. We were actually having a conversation about the importance of noticing the things around us when I failed to notice the police car inching up behind me. Since we were driving through this shore town in the off season, the roads were empty and I hadn't realized how fast I was driving. Heather still teases me about that ticket because I was so focused on our journey that I missed a significant detail – the police officer and his interest in my speed.

When I travel alone, I tend to choose a direct route from my starting point to my destination. When I take road trips with Heather, the route is never direct. Realizing that it is okay, and even beneficial, to veer off course has been a great learning experience for me. I tend to view my life in the same way, looking for the fastest route from Point A to Point B, but I know not everyone does this. Some people live in many different places and try out several jobs on their journey to the life they want to live. I admire these people. I think they are richer for these experiences. They understand that life is not a race and that there are many oddities to explore along the way.

When Heather and I took a trip to a cranberry bog in New Jersey, she planned many unrelated stops along the way. As usual, she didn't tell me the cranberry bog was the intended destination. When she picked me up that day she simply said, "There may be some off-road driving. Should we take your car or mine?" I don't mind driving, but if there is a chance of getting stuck in a ditch somewhere, I will happily volunteer her car. Before we ever reached the cranberry bog, we stopped to see a giant medical bag, a giant cowboy, some musical robots made of car parts, and some metallic statues made of gas cylinders!

We have so much fun when we stop at these secondary attractions. First, they are usually hard to find because they aren't really tourist attractions, they are oddities. We usually drive in circles and find ourselves doubled over in laughter before we even spot the oddity. And then there is often a spectacle as we stop to take pictures of the oddities. When other people see us pulling over with our cameras at the side of the road they wonder what is going on. I have learned when we pay attention to something, others will be curious and pay attention to it as well. This can be true in your everyday life also. Try telling people about your interests and see how the interest spreads! As we took pictures with the gas cylinder robots on that trip a few cars honked and the passengers waved to us. Also, there is nothing to lose on these side ventures. If we fail to find the oddity, it makes a good story. Once, even though we found the ceramic animals Heather had wanted to see, all the camera captured was darkness. If you pick up a new hobby, or take some time off from work to write a book, and nothing productive comes of your venture, just appreciate the diversion from your route. You will reach your destination eventually.

One place I highly recommend that has no admission charge is the Cape May County Zoo in New Jersey. This zoo is home to over 550 creatures from more than 250 different species. Although there is a petting zoo, this zoo and wildlife preserve also houses larger animals that you would expect to find at a zoo with a costly admission charge. There is an aviary filled with birds and there is a reptile house with everything from small lizards to alligators and giant tortoises. There are lions, and tigers, and bears. You can visit different continents within the zoo and meet everything from giraffes to capybara to bison. My children attended the summer camp at this zoo when they were small and I was amazed at the hands-on experience they had with these animals. They learned to make food and toys that were appreciated by the monkeys and bears. They were able to feed the giraffes. They were educated about the things a zoo does to keep the animals safe and happy. For example, one reptile enclosure was designed to minimize the noise from the visitors on the other side of the glass. The children at the camp were asked to enter an old enclosure and subjected to the camp counselor tapping on the glass from the outside. After hearing the awful sound that it makes in the enclosure, my children never wanted to tap the glass at an animal exhibit again.

What is the Pace of your Life?

Please rate the following statements based on your experience: N = never R = rarely S = sometimes O = often A = all the time					
	N	R	S	O	A
I get frustrated when people are walking slowly in front of me					
I skip meals if I am in a hurry					
I make decisions before I have all the facts					
I get upset when traffic moves slowly					
I use *fast forward* to skip commercials					
I send hasty text or email responses without taking time to think first					
I get frustrated when my checkout line moves slowly at a store					
People tell me that I speak fast					
I get frustrated when my internet destination is slow to load					

	N	R	S	O	A
I find myself wishing time would pass faster when I am at work					
I get impatient when service is slow at a restaurant					
I fill my daily schedule with activities					

To score this quiz :

Never=1, Rarely=2, Occasionally=3, Often=4, All the Time=5

Add up the boxes you checked to get a total score.

Now rate the pace of your life:

If you scored:

above 50: You move through life extremely quickly. You expect others to move quickly too. You are definitely missing things that could bring you joy.

45-49: You move through life very quickly. You have little patience for people who move slowly. You could be missing opportunities to find joy or improve your life.

40-44: You move through life quickly. You probably get a lot accomplished, but you might not be enjoying the ride.

35-39: You move through life at an average speed. As you go through your day make time to appreciate where you are without wanting to move.

30-34: You move through life slowly. You are probably taking time to savor your life. At your speed you may notice opportunities that others miss.

25-29: You move through life very slowly. You feel no need to rush and you are patient with others. Your Zen attitude may bring you happiness.

below 25: You move through life extremely slowly. It is wonderful that you are taking time to enjoy your life, but don't move so slowly that you get nothing accomplished. You may want to pick up the pace to revitalize your life.

Exercise 9: Finding your Pace

When you took the pace of life quiz, you may have found that you are often rushing. Many people find themselves rushing these days. Our advanced technologies make us expect instantaneous results and we often find our attention divided between multiple tasks. The problem with rushing is that when we do this we are not present; we are so focused on accomplishing the task that we are not really paying attention to the world around us. Rushing also produces a state of anxiety. Instead of getting ahead, the more we rush, the more we seem to lack. If you are a person who rushes, you will find that it frees up time, which you then fill with other activities, adding to an already full schedule.

Psychologists who study happiness and life satisfaction have learned that rushing mindlessly through life does not increase our life satisfaction. People who are happy with their lives tend to be people who devote time to things that they are passionate about rather than spending all of their time trying to be productive.

Mihaly Csikszentmihalyi, who studies creativity and happiness, developed a concept called "flow" to explain what happens when we immerse ourselves in a pleasurable activity. Csikszentmihalyi found that creative people get lost in the act of creating and become motivated by their own intrinsic drive to do the work, rather than extrinsic factors like payment or recognition. Even if you are not a creative person, you have experienced moments where you become so focused on the task at hand that you lose track of time. When time seems to disappear and you are just doing the activity for the sake of the activity, you are in a state of "flow." People who experience flow describe it as an experience of ecstasy, a state of being outside of your normal reality. The interesting thing about flow is that although the experience of flow is linked to increased happiness, you don't actually experience happiness while you are in a state of flow. While you are doing an activity that creates flow for you, you will feel no emotions; you are completely focused on the task at hand. For some people playing sports creates a state of flow. For others it is painting or drawing. You may lose track of time while having an engaging conversation. Or you may find yourself in a state of flow on a road trip.

According to Csikszentmihalyi, to achieve flow you must find the perfect balance of challenge and skill. If the task you are doing is too easy, meaning that your skill level is high and the challenge is low, then you won't care much about it and may not even give it your full attention. For example, people often get frustrated at work when they are given a trivial task to complete and they feel it is a waste of time. If the task is too difficult, meaning that your skill level is low and the challenge is high, then you will experience anxiety that will distract you from the moment. If your boss asks you to complete a project requiring skills you do not have or are not comfortable using, like new technology, then you may experience panic instead of flow. The perfect balance occurs when you have a strong skill set and you are also challenged by the task.

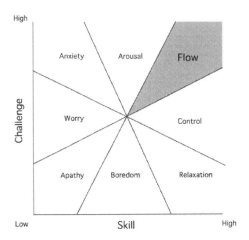

To get into a state of flow you can follow these steps:

1) **Choose a task where you have some skill**.
For me, working on a book is something I might choose because I know I have some ability to write and do research on my topic.

2) **Make sure the task is still challenging for you**.
Remember that if your skill set is high, but the task is too easy, you will feel relaxed and in control, but you will not experience flow. My challenge may be learning about a new topic, or finding the best way to communicate what I know about a topic to a reading audience.

3) **Have a specific goal in mind.**
You should not be working for an extrinsic reward, but you do want to have an idea of where the project is headed.

4) **Avoid interruptions.**
A call on your cell phone or a growling stomach can interrupt your state of flow, so try to make sure you will be working in a distraction-free environment.

5) **Give yourself some time.**
Remember that when you achieve a state of flow you can lose track of time, so don't try to achieve it when you have to be somewhere in 20 minutes. There is nothing worse than emerging from a state of flow and feeling blissful, only to realize you have missed an important commitment. Give yourself some time – you are worth it.

6) **Focus on the process and not the end state.**
Did you know that when young children first start scribbling with crayons, they don't even know they should be drawing *something*? It is not until we ask, "What are you drawing?" that they realize there is supposed to be a final product. Young children are drawing for the sake of drawing.

During the week that I was teaching my Positive Psychology class about the topic of flow, a large snowstorm dumped 24 inches of snow on my very long driveway. Too stubborn to hire a plow, I set out to shovel the driveway myself, and to my surprise (and delight) I experienced a state of flow. I completely lost track of time as more and more blacktop appeared behind me. When the task was complete, I was very sore, but also very content. As other storms followed that season, I began to refer to the time I spent on my driveway as "shoveling meditation."

≈≈≈ REWARDED WITH A VISTA

One of the goals of a road trip with Heather is to end up in a beautiful place that brings us happiness. When she proposed we take a trip to Point Pleasant, New Jersey, she explained her destination choice saying, "I saw a picture of a Tiki Bar in Point Pleasant and thought *I would like to find myself there at the end of the day looking out at that view.*" We talked about that trip and that Tiki Bar for several weeks before the trip actually happened. Anticipating an event generates happiness; this is why the mere act of planning a road trip can make you happy, even if you never take the trip.

When we finally found an evening that we were both free to drive to the Tiki Bar, we did not follow a straight route there. We made many stops on the way to Point Pleasant. We looked forward to our relaxing drink by the beach as we searched for paranormal photo opportunities and met with a psychic. When we finally arrived at the bar we chose a seat on the second floor, looking over the boardwalk and out into the ocean. It was a beautiful view, and a wonderful way to end the day.

A "vista" is a spectacular view, an outlook or a perspective. There is a park in Connecticut, not far from where I went to college called the Devil's Hopyard. The Devil's Hopyard has woods and hiking trails. One theory about the park's name is that it refers to the unexplained dents in the rocks along the creek at this park. An urban legend claims that as the devil moved through the creek his tail made dents in the rocks. The dented rocks are not far from the parking area. However, if you want a spectacular view, you need to hike a while until you reach Vista Point. Vista Point is located at the end of the blue hiking trail in the Devil's Hopyard and it stands about 150 feet above the Eightmile River. You have to hike for about one and a half miles through woods, along creeks, and up steep inclines before being rewarded with a beautiful view of the valley below. I appreciate the fact that you have to work to achieve that view. On the day I went with Heather, the park was full of people. We ended up ascending a skinny trail to the vista with a large group of tourists and we all arrived at the vista at the same time. It was hard to get a clear camera shot of the view without including tourists in the picture. However, when the tourists moved, we were rewarded with a beautiful vista.

Just up the road from the Devil's Hopyard you can visit Gillette Castle. Gillette Castle was a home owned by William Gillette, an actor who played Sherlock Holmes in the theater. Gillette loved mystery and surprises, and on a tour of the castle you can learn about all of the tricks and puzzles he built into his home. For example, many cabinets in his home had elaborate puzzles a person needed to complete in order to open them. One of these puzzles was on his liquor cabinet, and he installed secret mirrors in his home that allowed him to leave the room and watch his dinner guests struggle to open the liquor cabinet. Behind the castle you will find a patio with a gorgeous view of the Connecticut River.

There are beautiful views near Heather's college too. If you visit Monticello, which means "Little Mountain" you will find scenic vistas of the country-side surrounding what was once the home of Thomas Jefferson. He lived there from 1770 until his death in 1826. It was on a tour of the Jefferson home that we learned the synchronicity story associated with Thomas Jefferson's death. Thomas Jefferson and John Adams (the president who preceded Jefferson) both died on the same day, July 4th, 1826. Adams died at the age of 90 in Quincy, Massachusetts while Jefferson, age 83, died at his home in Monticello, Virginia. Both men had signed the Declaration of Independence, and as they lay dying, America celebrated the 50th anniversary of this declaration. As the story goes, the last words spoken by Adams on his deathbed were, "Jefferson still lives." He could not have known that Jefferson had died just hours earlier.

There are many places to enjoy a vista in the Shenandoah Valley in Virginia. When you drive along the

Skyline Drive in Virginia, you can pull over at several locations to appreciate the view. Skyline Drive is a 109-mile road that runs the entire length of the Shenandoah National Park in the Blue Ridge Mountains. It is accessible from four main entrances off major Virginia highways. There are similar vistas on an ascending highway at Acadia National Park in Maine. Heather and I have made that trip with our grandparents and our Aunt Barbara. There is a part of Acadia Park called Schoodic Point that was one of my grandfather's favorite places on Earth. He loved to sit on the rocks and look out over the sea. My Aunt Barbara made sure to get him to that vista even when he was no longer able to drive.

On some of our trips, we found views that were more interesting than expansive. One of these locations was Foamhenge in Natural Bridge, Virginia. In this park, you can find a replica of Stonehenge made of Styrofoam. It is a rewarding view because the large structures make you feel like you are in the presence of something amazing, even though the Styrofoam makes you appreciate the ridiculousness of the park. Admission to the exhibit was free and the opportunities for fun pictures were plentiful.

We found similar structures at a park called Columcille Megalith Park in Bangor, Pennsylvania. Here, the structures were made of stone. The sculptures in this park were inspired by formations found on the Isle of Iona, off the coast of Scotland. Once again, Heather managed to find exotic scenes in our own backyard.

Most people believe that a life well lived will lead to

rewards, whether you receive them in this life or the next. Heather and I definitely look forward to the rewards that come at the end of our road trips. Many of our road trips include amazing vistas that justify the journey. When we stop and appreciate these vistas, they remind us to live in the present moment and to have gratitude for the gifts that we have in our lives. However, the vista is not usually the only reward on these road trips. We like to joke that our road trips must end with Italian food and a pitcher of Sangria. In reality, the trips may end up anywhere, with a variety of foods and beverages. On one trip, returning home from New Jersey we stopped for Sangria and had a conversation about who would drink and who would drive home. Heather decided to drive so I could drink. As we were on our way home my cell phone rang. Right after I answered it, I hung up on the caller and exclaimed, "I can't be on the phone while I am driving in New Jersey!" Heather laughed and reminded me that she was driving. Sometimes the reward at the end of the road trip is just allowing someone else to take the wheel.

A vista provides a new perspective. One of the great rewards of a road trip is that it can change your perspective. Getting away from your everyday life makes things novel and draws your attention to the present moment. As you change your perspective, you may be more likely to notice synchronicity in your life. Opportunities may present themselves when you keep your eyes on the road. Trying new things on a road trip may help you find what you are passionate about. Taking chances on a road trip may encourage you to pursue your big dreams. Being on a road trip allows you to leave your troubles behind and focus on the things you are grateful for. Being brave on a road trip allows you to overcome your fears. You can broaden your perspective and see other routes to your destination. You can see the world from someone else's perspective when you put yourself into their world. You can learn to listen. You can try different paces. You can find your best possible outcome.

According to Tal Ben-Shar, a Positive Psychology professor at Harvard:

"Attaining lasting happiness requires that we enjoy the journey on our way toward a destination we deem valuable. Happiness is not about making it to the peak of the mountain nor is it about climbing aimlessly around the mountain; happiness is the experience of climbing toward the peak"

As we journey through life, all of us are looking for moments where life is beautiful and we are happy. When we achieve this, I call it the Best Possible Outcome. There are many paths you can take to get to your best possible outcome, and what is best for you at one moment may no longer be the best at another time. All of the earlier chapters in this book are roads that can lead you to your Best Possible Outcome.

Have you Achieved Your Best Possible Outcome?

Please rate the following statements based on your experience:

SD = Strongly Disagree   D = Disagree   A = Agree   SA = Strongly Agree

	SD	D	Not Sure	A	SA
I am working at the best possible job for me (include unemployed as a job option)					
I am in the best possible romantic relationship for me (include single as a relationship option)					
I have the best possible living arrangement for me					
I am currently at the optimum health for me					
I am able to travel as much as I want to					
I spend as much time on my hobbies as I want to					
I am comfortable with the amount of time I devote to spiritual practice					
I am making good progress toward achieving my goals					

	SD	D	Not Sure	A	SA
I forgive myself for bad decisions I made in the past					
I have people who love me					
I know where to find resources when I need them					
My appearance reflects who I am					

To score this quiz :

SD =1, D =2, Not Sure =3, A=4, SA =5

Add up the boxes you checked to get a total score.

Now rate your experience with living your best possible life:

If you scored:

above 50: You are living your best possible life. You are a person who understands "the power of now" and you appreciate everything you have.

45-49: You are very close to your best possible life. Before you make good changes, take some time to appreciate what is good in your current life.

40-44: You are close to living your best possible life. There are a few things you would like to change, but most things in your life are going well.

35-39: You have an average level of contentment with your life. There are many things that work for you, but there are some things you would like to improve. Focus on the positive first and then ask yourself how you can bring the other facets of your life up to speed.

30-34: You not living your best possible life. You may not know what you want out of life. Take some time to imagine what your best possible life would look like.

25-29: You are really not living your best possible life. You may be trying to uphold someone else's standards, or live the life others expect for you. Take some time to think about what YOU want.

below 25: You are not living your best possible life. You seem defeated. If your life is not what you want, make some drastic changes and start moving toward your best possible life.

Exercise 10: Living your Best Possible Life

After taking the best possible outcome quiz, you may have a better idea of the areas in your life where you are reaping rewards and the areas of your life where you would like to improve. There are many paths to your Best Possible Outcome. The field of Positive Psychology is currently focused on not only the things that bring us happiness, but the things that lead us to a life of well-being or flourishing. According to the man credited with founding Positive Psychology, Martin Seligman, the formula for flourishing is PERMA:

Positive emotions
Engagement
Relationships
Meaning
Achievement

Positive emotions include feelings of pleasure, love and joy. Life is better when we are experiencing positive emotions. Engagement is the state of flow you experience when your level of skill matches the challenge of your task. Having strong personal relationships enhances the quality of our lives. Finding meaning in our lives contributes to our life satisfaction. Achievement can make us feel that our life has been worthwhile.

As you read through this book you should have seen how a road trip includes all aspects of PERMA. You will experience positive emotions from the moment you begin to plan your road trip. You may experience engagement (flow) in the planning of the trip or in the road trip itself. Road trips can enhance your relationships by deepening your connection to your road trip companions, or introducing you to new people you meet on the road. A road trip can enhance the meaning in your life in several ways; the activities you incorporate into your trip may be meaningful, or the time on a road trip may give you an opportunity to identify and appreciate the things that are meaningful in your everyday life. Finally, there is a sense of achievement when you complete the road trip you have planned. Having success with that trip may increase your confidence that you can be successful in other endeavors in your life.

What is Your Best Possible Outcome?

Your Best Possible Outcome is unique to you and it is not a fixed outcome. Only you know when you are living the life that is best for you. Everyone has experienced moments when everything seems to be falling into place. These are moments when you are reaching your Best Possible Outcome. The goal of this book is to help you experience more of these moments.

A Clarification and Caution about Best Possible Outcomes

It is important to note that I do not intend for the Best Possible Outcome to be your final destination. The Best

Possible Outcome quiz should give you a "You Are Here" marker for the map of your life. Just as the end of a road trip is the final destination for a trip, but may not be the last place you ever go, your Best Possible Outcome can change throughout your life. What is "best" for you today may not be "best" for you tomorrow.

As Shawn Achor points out in *The Happiness Advantage*, when people achieve a goal, they rarely stop and say, "I am happy now." It is more likely that they set a new goal. He argues that this is why we cannot say, "When I achieve my goal, I will be happy." There will always be another goal.

Daniel Gilbert cautions that we don't actually know what will make us happy. We base decisions about what will make us happy in the future on the things that will make us happy now. This is true on a road trip too. Maybe a large stack of pancakes sounds fantastic as you leave for your trip, but when you reach your destination, you may be craving Italian food. Gilbert also found that having more choices does not necessarily make us happier. When Heather shows up for a road trip she does not ask, "Where would you like to go today?" She already has the trip mapped out. Gilbert says if we are given many options we will never be completely satisfied with the one we chose, but if we are not given a choice, we come to love the one we got.

To Achieve your Best Possible Outcome

On a road trip from Philadelphia to Boston, my friend Kyle taught me a road trip game called "Paddidle." To play the game, you must shout "Paddidle!" whenever you see a car with a head light that is out. The first one to shout "Paddidle!" wins that round. I had never heard of that game before, and I had never really paid much attention to missing headlights. Now that I know the game, I see missing headlights everywhere, and every time I see one, I catch myself saying, "Padiddle."

Now that you have read a book about road trips, you might start hearing about road trips all the time. Just as I say "Paddidle" every time I see a missing headlight, I would encourage you to pause every time you hear the word "road" or "trip." If you encounter either of these words throughout your day, you should stop what you are doing and focus on something that you are grateful for at that moment. If you hear the words "road" and "trip" together, you probably have at least two things you can express gratitude for! Being aware of the good things you already have in your life will help you focus on attracting more of what you want into your life.

≈≈≈ ABOUT THE QUIZZES IN THIS BOOK

I created the quizzes in this book to measure the constructs addressed in each chapter. Many years of experience conducting research and teaching research methods to college students prepared me for the creation of these quizzes.

To assess the validity of the quizzes, a group of 52 people ages 19 to 32 volunteered to complete all ten quizzes. Before completing the quizzes they each rated their belief about how they would perform in each category. If the quizzes in this book are accurately measuring the trait in the quiz title, then the student ratings should correlate with the quiz scores. For example, someone who rates themselves high on gratitude should receive a high score on the gratitude quiz. All of the correlations, except the pace of life measure, were significant, meaning that the score they received on the quiz matched their self-rating.

I used a statistic called Pearson's r to evaluate the relationship between self-assessments of each trait and the corresponding quiz scores. The Pearson's r provides a number that describes the relationship between the two measures. The range of possible Pearson r values is 0 – 1, where 0 represents no relationship between the two tests and 1 represents a perfect relationship between the two tests. The closer the r value is to 1, the stronger the relationship between the two tests. A strong relationship suggests that the quiz is accurately measuring the construct. For a comparison using 52 people, the relationship must be greater than r = .27 to be considered a significant relationship. Correlations below .27 would not indicate a relationship between the two tests. Below I have ranked the constructs for how well quiz scores matched people's self-evaluations. The number in the parentheses is the Pearson's r statistic.

Match between Self-Assessments and Quiz Scores

Ability to Listen (.74)
Passion for Life (.70)
Fear (.64)
Personal Relationships (.63)
Life Satisfaction (.50)
Synchronicity (.39)
Gratitude (.38)
Flexibility (.32)
Big Dreams (.29)

Pace of life measures did not correlate with each other. This could mean that people do poorly at estimating the pace of their lives, or that there are problems with the pace of life quiz I created. Further analysis of the pace of life quiz was required and will be discussed at the end of this chapter.

The overall quiz results from the 52 people surveyed yielded the following data:

Synchronicity
RANGE = 19-43   AVERAGE = 31 (+/- 6 points)
Most synchronicity scores fell between 25-37.

Passion for Life
RANGE = 29-60   AVERAGE = 49 (+/- 6 points)
Most passion for life scores fell between 43-55.

Big Dreams:
RANGE = 27-59   AVERAGE = 47 (+/- 7 points)
Most big dreams scores fell between 40-54.

Gratitude
RANGE = 34-60   AVERAGE = 51 (+/- 6 points)
Most gratitude scores fell between 45-57.

Fear
RANGE = 12-55   AVERAGE = 33 (+/- 10 points)
Most fear scores fell between 23-43.

Flexibility (Willingness to Change)
RANGE = 34-60   AVERAGE = 47 (+/- 6 points)
Most flexibility scores fell between 41-53.

Personal Relationships
RANGE = 30-57   AVERAGE = 45 (+/- 6 points)
Most personal relationship scores fell between 39-51.

Ability to Listen
RANGE = 35-60   AVERAGE = 49 (+/- 7 points)
Most ability to listen scores fell between 42-56.

Pace of Life
RANGE = 26-54   AVERAGE = 41 (+/- 6 points)
Most pace of life scores fell between 35-47.

Living your Best Possible Life
RANGE = 29-57   AVERAGE = 41 (+/- 6 points)
Most best possible life scored fell between 35-47.

Take a moment to look at the scores you received on each of the quizzes. How do your test results compare with these averages? Do you fall within the typical range for most of the quizzes, or do you have some areas where you scored extremely low or extremely high?

The Pearson statistic can also be used to investigate the relationship between these constructs. For example, is there a relationship between your score on the gratitude test and your score on the test that measured whether you are living your best possible life? Again, the scores of the 52 volunteers were used to assess the relationship between the ten constructs. Below you will find a quick guide to the traits that are related. The order of traits in each lists reflects the strength of the relationship.

Synchronicity is significantly related to:
    Relationships
    Living Your Best Possible Life
    Gratitude

Passion for Life is significantly related to:
    Gratitude
    Big Dreams
    Flexibility
    Living Your Best Possible Life
    Relationships
    Listening
Passion is negatively related to Fear, meaning that higher levels of passion are associated with lower levels of fear.

Big Dreams is significantly related to:
    Gratitude
    Passion
    Flexibility
    Living Your Best Possible Life
    Relationships
Big Dreams are negatively related to Fear, meaning that

people who have big dreams show lower levels of fear.

Gratitude is significantly related to:

    Passion

    Big Dreams

    Living Your Best Possible Life

    Flexibility

    Relationships

    Listening

    Synchronicity

Gratitude is negatively related to Fear, meaning that higher levels of gratitude are associated with lower levels of fear.

Fear demonstrates a *negative* relationship with:

    Passion

    Gratitude

    Big Dreams

    Flexibility

    Living Your Best Possible Life

This suggests that high levels of fear are associated with lower scores for passion, gratitude, having big dreams, being flexible, and living your best possible life.

Flexibility is significantly related to:

    Big Dreams

    Passion

    Gratitude

    Living Your Best Possible Life

    Listening

Flexibility is negatively related to Fear, meaning that higher levels of fear are associated with lower levels of flexibility.

Relationships are significantly related to:
Listening
Passion
Gratitude
Living Your best Possible Life
Synchronicity
Big Dreams

Listening is significantly related to:
Relationships
Flexibility
Living Your Best Possible Life
Gratitude
Passion

Living Your Best Possible Life is significantly related to:
Gratitude
Passion
Big Dreams
Flexibility
Relationships
Synchronicity
Listening

Living your best possible life is negatively related to Fear, meaning that people who have high levels of life satisfaction are people who have lower levels of fear.

Tables Showing Correlations for the Ten Traits

(only significant correlation values are shown)

	Sync	Passion	Dreams	Gratitude	Fear
Synchronicity	1.00	---	---	.283	---
Passion	---	1.00	.671	.744	-.622
Big Dreams	---	.671	1.00	.698	-.597
Gratitude	.283	.744	.698	1.00	-.604
Fear	---	-.622	-.597	-.604	1.00
Flexibilty	---	.552	.566	.482	-.404
Relationships	.338	.490	.315	.479	---
Listening	---	.282	---	.299	---
Pace of Life	---	---	---	---	---
Best Possible	.313	.492	.483	.558	-.339

	Flex	Relations	Listen	Pace	Best Outcome
Synchronicity	---	.338	---	---	.313
Passion	.552	.490	..282	---	.492
Big Dreams	.566	.315	---	---	.483
Gratitude	.482	.479	.299	---	.558
Fear	-.404	---	---	---	-.339
Flexibilty	1.00	---	.319	---	.421
Relationships	---	1.00	.628	---	.403
Listening	.319	.628	1.00	---	.302
Pace of Life	---	---	---	1.00	---
Best Possible	.421	..403	.302	---	1.00

The pace of your life quiz did not correlate with any of the other constructs in this dataset. I had expected people who move quickly through life to be less satisfied with their lives overall. A Taoist proverb proclaims "We cannot see our reflection in running water." I surmised it would be hard to do the self-analysis required for growth if a person is moving through life too fast. However, the data from these 52 volunteers showed no relationship between the pace of life and living your best possible life. This lack of relationship combined with the fact that self-assessments of pace of your life did not match scores on the pace of life quiz led me to conclude that the pace of life measure had some problems.

I wanted to make sure that this book included accurate measurements of each construct to evaluate your progress, so I conducted some further analysis on the pace of life quiz. I was able to identify pace of life questions within the quiz that were not showing a reliable relationship to other pace of life questions. The pace of life quiz that appears in this book has been updated to eliminate questions that did not accurately measure the pace of life. For example, "I drive faster than the speed limit" and "I set an alarm to wake me up on my days off" involve other personality characteristics not necessarily related to a preferred pace of life. It is possible that people who tend to move quickly through life may not drive faster than the speed limit because they don't want to get a ticket! These questions were changed to "I get upset when traffic moves slowly" and "I fill my daily schedule with activities."

The updated pace of life quiz was given to 40 people and the scores on the pace of life quiz now matched self-assessments of pace of life (.46). This suggests that the new quiz is doing a better job measuring "pace of life." It is interesting to note that the new quiz also showed a negative relationship to the quiz measuring living your best possible life (-.39). This is in line with what I was expecting. People who move quickly through life tend to be less satisfied with their lives overall.

≈≈≈ CONCLUSION

According to the data collected from the quizzes, living your best possible life is most highly related to being grateful. There are many levels of gratitude: you can appreciate the greater world around you, you can be grateful for the blessings you have in your life, and you can appreciate the things you have personally achieved. Taking road trips can enhance your experience of all three types of gratitude. When you explore a new location, you can appreciate the beauty in nature, or even man-made design. You can be grateful that you have the time for a road trip, the vehicle to take the trip, and possibly the companionship of a person who will take the journey with you. You can also feel grateful for the lessons you learn on your trip and the improvements to the quality of your life that may come from taking that road trip.

Living your best possible life is also highly correlated with having a passion for life. If you are not feeling excited about your life, a road trip is a great way to kick-start that passion. Often passion starts with curiosity. What are you curious about? What would you like to learn more about? Plan a road trip to explore the things you are curious about.

Another thing that correlates with living your best possible life is having big dreams. Big dreams are plans, things you want to achieve. Planning road trips gives you a chance to practice setting goals and achieving them.

Living your best possible life is also related to a willingness to change your course. Road trips with Heather often involved a change of course. By taking road trips, you can develop your ability to recognize when you are going the wrong way and strengthen your willingness to turn around. You can then bring this strength back to your everyday life to help you live your best possible life.

The strength of your personal connections is also related to the likelihood that you will live your best possible life. Taking a road trip with someone can strengthen that relationship. You may also make new personal connections on your journey. Even if you take your road trip alone and don't speak to another person, getting comfortable with yourself will go a long way in helping you to connect with others. If you like spending all day in a car with yourself, surely someone else will too.

Synchronicity was a new concept for some of the people who took these quizzes, but everyone could relate to the scenarios described in the synchronicity quiz. Based on the results, the experience of synchronicity, being able to recognize meaningful coincidences, is correlated with living your best possible life. Because a road trip is a novel experience, you are likely to be paying attention, and are more likely to recognize these meaningful coincidences when they occur. I think people who experience synchronicity are closer to living their best possible life because they see and take advantage of opportunities when they arise. Synchronicities also create a feeling of wonder and awe, which may lead to gratitude, and gratitude is the quality that correlated the highest with living your best possible life.

The last thing that significantly correlated with living your best possible life was the ability to listen. People who listen will learn things that can improve the quality of their lives. Listening is most highly correlated with the strength of personal relationships. This is not surprising because part of making a human connection is listening to the person you would like to connect with. Personal connections are a very important part of living your best possible life.

One thing that did not correlate with any of the other variables was the pace of your life. If the pace of your life is not related to living your best possible life this would be an interesting and exciting outcome. It would mean the pace of your road trip shouldn't matter at all. I recently had a conversation with a friend who claimed that the hiking I do isn't "real" hiking because I don't camp out when I hike. A few days later he read an article about downhill skiing versus cross-country skiing and he realized that they are two different things and you can't conclude that one is more "real" due to the pace. He realized that although he likes to cover distance so he can set up a camp for the night, I enjoy hiking just for the sake of the hike, and neither one is more "real." However, when the pace of life quiz was fixed to better capture the construct, it *did* correlate with living your best possible life, as predicted. It appears that moving through life quickly leads people to be less satisfied with their lives.

The only thing that showed a negative relationship to living your best possible life was fear. Heather and I often experienced situations that generated fear on our road trips. Heather has told me that she often seeks out scary experiences for our road trips because she believes that I enjoy them, even though she does not. She says that when she experiences these fearful things with me she knows everything will be alright. So, the idea of a road trip is not necessarily to generate fear, but to conquer your fears. By getting rid of fear, you will get closer to living your best possible life.

In his book, *The Happiness Advantage*, Shawn Achor recommends seven things that can instantly improve your happiness:

    1) meditation
    2) anticipation
    3) doing acts of kindness
    4) creating a positive environment
    5) exercise
    6) spending money on others/experiences
    7) expressing a strength of character

When Heather plans a road trip she incorporates all of these things. Meditation involves focused attention and calming the mind. People who are skilled at meditation may experience a state of flow when they meditate. Heather is able to engage in driving meditation and hiking meditation on our road trips.

Research shows that the anticipation of a reward can make us happier than the reward itself. Planning a road trip allows Heather to anticipate the journey and the destinations. As you may have realized reading this book, road trips may not always turn out the way you planned. However, that is not a problem when much of the joy comes from the anticipation of the journey.

Heather's life could be defined by her acts of kindness. She is truly the most generous person I know. When Heather plans a road trip she is careful to consider the needs and desires of her companions, and she is kind to everyone she meets along the way.

On a road trip, Heather creates a positive environment by bringing a positive attitude and a smile. She often plans music, games, food and/or comfort items, depending on the duration of the trip.

Although much of a road trip is spent sitting in a car, Heather usually builds a physical activity into the adventure. Climbing mountains and running from ghosts can release endorphins that make you happy.

Heather knows that the secret to spending money well is to spend it on others and on experiences. In his book, *Luxury Fever*, Robert Frank explains that people who are given money to spend on someone else feel happier after making the purchase than people given money to spend on themselves. He also finds that people who spend money on things experience a short burst of happiness, but people who spend money on experiences maintain the happiness longer as they replay the experience over in their minds.

Finally, some of Heather's greatest strengths include humor and kindness. Heather finds a way to express her generosity and make me laugh on every road trip we take!

Through road trips, Heather has clearly found all of the keys to happiness. Happiness is a good feeling, but it differs from life satisfaction, which I would argue is more substantial. I believe that Heather's road trips have also taught me the keys to life satisfaction, or a life well-lived. The life lessons I learned from taking road trips with Heather include:

1) Coincidences can be meaningful
2) It is important to be excited about your life
3) It is okay to aim high
4) There is so much to be grateful for
5) Fear can be overcome
6) There is more than one way to get to your goal
7) People matter
8) It is important to pay attention
9) Don't waste time rushing
10) It can be a wonderful life

When you are aware of these ten things and use them to enhance the quality of your life, you will be moving closer toward your best possible outcome. It is my hope that the stories and exercises in this book will help you on your journey.

One of my friends who read *The Secret* by Rhonda Byrne said, "This book will change your life…at least for a week or two…and then you'll forget and go back to your normal life." This book may be like that too. You might put the exercises into practice for a while and then slip back into your familiar patterns. However, the good news is that now you know what to do anytime you get into a rut and forget all the wisdom you gained from reading this book and completing the exercises – take a road trip!

Recently, I took a trip to the supermarket to buy groceries. That does not fit my definition of a road trip. As I drove I noticed the clouds above me. It had stormed the night before and the dark gray clouds were giving way to the bright white clouds. The sun was peeking through the clouds. Rain drops glistened on my windshield. There was no snow, unusual for January in Pennsylvania, but everything was beautiful. I realized that I like seeing the world through my windshield. It occurred to me that when I drive, I have to keep my eyes open. A road trip keeps you mindful and in the moment because driving *requires that you are mindful and in the moment*. Even the trips I *have* to take have become more meaningful. Thank you, Heather.

ODDITIES TO INSPIRE YOUR ROAD TRIPS

The following attractions were mentioned in this book. Other great oddities can be found by searching Roadside America online. Photos taken by Heather Hampel.

Assateague
Maryland Beach inhabited by feral horses.
7206 National Seashore Lane, Berlin, MD 21811

Bushkill Falls
A series of eight waterfalls and variety of trails and bridges that vary in length and difficulty
Bushkill Falls Road, Bushkill, PA 18324

The Candle Shoppe of the Poconos

The upstairs is a quaint candle shop, and the basement
is a haunted attraction.
1900 PA-611, Swiftwater, PA 18370

Cape May County Zoo

Over 250 species inhabit this free zoo near the beach.
Cape May Courthouse, NJ 08210

Car Shop in Natural Bridge
We found this by accident as we drove up a mountain behind the
Natural Bridge Museum.
Natural Bridge, VA 24578

Chincoteague National Wildlife Refuge
Provides a habitat for birds, wildlife, plants and the Chincoteague
Ponies.
8231 Beach Rd, Chincoteague Island, VA 23336

Circus Town Diner

Historic, circus-themed hub serving burgers and more with car-hop service or at tables under a big top.
1861 NJ-35, Wall Township, NJ 07719

Columcille Megalith Park

Inspired by the Isle of Iona off the coast of Scotland this park features stone formations creating a place of mystery and spirituality.
2155 Fox Gap Rd, Bangor, PA 18013

Daniel Boone Homestead

The childhood home of American Frontiersman Daniel Boone. Includes historic buildings, trails, picnic areas, and a lake. (We are standing by the Saw Mill).
400 Daniel Boone Road, Birdsboro, PA 19508

Foamhenge

A full-size replica of Stonehenge made entirely out of Styrofoam.
Hwy 11 South, Natural Bridge, VA 24578

Giant Barbell

Giant dumbbells make a great photo opportunity, behind a gym equipment store
122 Southeast End Blvd; Quakertown, PA 18951

Gillette Castle

A castle full of tricks and mystery built by William Hooker Gillette, the actor who played Sherlock Holmes.
67 River Rd, East Haddam, CT 06423

The Haines Shoe House

Built in 1948, the shoe-shaped house offers guided tours, gift shop, ice cream & tasty treats for your enjoyment.
197 Shoe House Rd, York, PA 17406

Huge Doctor's Bag with Stethoscope

Apex Medical Center
537 Stanton Christiana Road, Newark DE 19713

Haunted Monster Museum (no longer open)

A spooky, formerly-abandoned Victorian manor built in the 1890's with fiberglass ghouls made by Mark Cline.
Hwy 130 and US 11, Natural Bridge, VA 24578

Hopewell Furnace

A colonial era plantation village, an example of an American 19th century rural iron plantation.
2 Mark Bird Ln, Elverson, PA 19520

La Bree's Bakery

Family-owned business featuring the most delicious un-iced home-style baked goods.
69 Gilman Falls Ave, Old Town, ME 04468

Manatawny Creek Winery

A family winery on a 90-acre farm in Amityville, Pennsylvania along the banks of the Manatawny Creek.
227 Levengood Rd, Douglassville, PA 19518

Martell's Tiki Bar
Funky beachfront dance club with tropical drinks, raised deck, views of the ocean & live band stage
308 Boardwalk, Point Pleasant Beach, NJ 08742

Mighty Joe Gorrilla
A giant gorilla statue at Mighty Joe's Gas, Grill and Deli.
1231 US Hwy 206, Shamong, NJ 08088

Monticello
Home of Thomas Jefferson.
931 Thomas Jefferson Pkwy, Charlottesville, VA 22902

Movie House: Amityville Horror
We drove by at 1am to find several trash bins at the end of the driveway marked with the address in blood-red paint.
18 Brooks Road, Toms River, NJ 08753

Muffler Man – Mr. Bill

This Muffler Man can be found at Mr. Bill's Ice Cream Stand, which was closed when we visited.
453 NJ-73, Hammonton, NJ 08037

Muffler Man – Rodeo Cowboy

This 22 ft. tall Cowboy Muffler Man is the mascot of the Cowtown Rodeo and Farmer's Market.
780 Hwy 40, Woodstown, NJ 08098

Musical Robots

Colorful robots made from auto parts displayed at Ralph's Auto Parts.
1011 Hwy 54, Buena, NJ 08310

Old Town Canoe (this building on Middle Street is gone)

Historic hub for one of Maine's most recognizable brands
The new store can be found at:
125 Gilman Falls Ave, Old Town, ME 04468

Oley Turnpike Dairy

Diner and ice cream along with a small zoo that features, goats and llamas.

6213 Oley Turnpike Road, Oley, PA 19547

Peg-leg Pirate Statue

The over 20 feet tall peg-legged, sword-wielding mascot of a water park.

10000 Hamilton Blvd, Breinigsville, PA 18031

Pink Cadillac Diner

Nostalgia-themed eatery featuring American comfort food, 1950s decor & a vintage car outside.
4347 S Lee Hwy, Natural Bridge, VA 24578

Rehoboth Beach

A diverse beachside community with charm and character.
1 Rehoboth Ave, Rehoboth Beach, DE 19971

Rockbridge Vineyard

A family-run winery in the beautiful Shenandoah Valley.
35 Hillview Ln, Raphine, VA 24472

Saint Peters Village

Historic buildings repurposed into shops including an inn, bakery, general store, creamery and boarding house. Hike the woods and visit the railroad trestle bridge over French Creek. See the remnants of the iron shaft mine and granite quarry that once supported the town.
3471 Saint Peters Road St. Peters Village, PA 19470

Shenandoah Caverns

Stunning underground caverns and a gift shop.
261 Caverns Rd, Quicksburg, VA 22847

Skyline Drive

A 109-mile road that runs the entire length of the Shenandoah
National Park in the Blue Ridge Mountains.

Accessible via 4 main entrances off major highways.

Turkey Hill Experience – Giant Cow

See a giant ceramic cow, learn how ice cream is made, and create your own flavor.
301 Linden St, Columbia, PA 17512

Wax Museum in Natural Bridge (permanently closed)

Life-sized figurines and scenes from Virginia's history.
70 Wert Faulkner Hwy, Natural Bridge Station, VA 24579

Whispering Wall

A curved stone wall that will transport your whisper from one end to the other.
University of Virginia, Charlottesville, VA 22901

Whitesbog Village & Cranberry Bog

Historic Village, General Store and a driving tour through the sand roads of the cranberry bog.
120 W Whites Bogs Rd #34, Browns Mills, NJ 08015

No pictures taken at these attractions:

It can't walk away on its own, but the owner of a giant ant sculpture [above] outside Allison Pest Control on Route 34, may have to take down the display unless he can get a variance from the Wall Township Board of Adjustment.

Alison Pest Control
The giant ant advertising the residential and commercial pest control business was removed before we got there.
1675 Hwy 34, Wall Township, NJ 07727

Acadia National Park
A 47,000-acre Atlantic coast recreation area primarily on Maine's Mount Desert Island. The landscape includes woods, rocky beaches and granite peaks. The wildlife includes moose, bear, whales, and seabirds.
Bar Harbor, ME 04609

Black Walnut Winery
Started by two couples who turned a hobby into a career, this winery uses grapes from neighboring vineyards to produce eighteen varietals and blends
3000 Lincoln Highway, Sadsburyville, PA 19320

The Cheese Shop
The Cheese Shop offers cheeses, specialty foods and a wine cellar. Enjoy a renowned "Cheese Shop" sandwich, cheese plate, and glass of wine on the patio.
410 W Duke of Gloucester St, Williamsburg, VA 23185

The Devil's Hopyard

Named for mysterious indents in the rocks along the falls, this scenic park offers hiking, stream fishing, bird watching, bicycling, picnicking and camping.
366 Hopyard Rd, East Haddam, CT 06423

Marsh Creek State Park

Marsh Creek State Park is a 1,705 acres Pennsylvania state park in Upper Uwchlan and Wallace Townships, Chester County, Pennsylvania in the United States. The park is the location of the 535-acre man-made Marsh Creek Lake.
675 Park Rd, Downingtown, PA 19335

Natural Bridge

A geological formation carved out of a gorge in the limestone forming an arch.
15 Appledore Lane, Natural Bridge, VA 24578

West Chester Ghost Tour

A popular walking tour of the West Chester borough that includes tales of ghosts, folklore and history, every Friday and Saturday night in October.
28 West Market Street, West Chester, PA 19380

BOOKS TO INSPIRE YOUR JOURNEY

Achor, Shawn. (2010). *The Happiness Advantage: The Seven Principles of Positive Psychology That Fuel Success and Performance at Work.* New York: Crown Business.

Byrne, Rhonda. (2006) *The Secret.* New York: Atria Books.

Csikszentmihalyi, Mihaly.(1990) *Flow: The Psychology of Optimal Experience.* New York: HarperCollins.

Emmons, Robert. (2007). *Thanks: How the New Science of Gratitude Can Make You Happier.* Boston: Houghton Mifflin Company.

Frank, Robert. (2000). *Luxury Fever.* New York: Princeton University Press.

Frankl, Victor. (2000). *Man's Search for Meaning.* New York: Simon & Schuster, Inc.

Gilbert, Daniel. (2006). *Stumbling on Happiness.* New York: Alfred A. Knopf.

Gilbert, Elizabeth. (2015). *Big Magic: Creative Living Beyond Fear.* New York: Riverhead Books.

Klosterman, Chuck. (2005). *Killing Yourself to Live: 85% of True Story.* New York: Scribner.

Langer, Ellen. (2009). *Counterclockwise: Mindful Health and the Power of Possibility*. New York: Ballantine.

Lyubomirsky, Sonja. (2007). *The How of Happiness: A New Approach to Getting the Life You Want*. New York: The Penguin Press.

Marcia, J., Waterman, A.S., Matteson, D.R., Archer, S.L., and Orlofsky, J.L. (1993). *Ego Identity: A Handbook for Psychosocial Research*. New York: Springer-Verlag.

Maslow, Abraham. (2011). *Toward a Psychology of Being: Reprint of 1962 Edition*. Eastford, CT: Martino Publishing.

McGee, Paul. (2013). *How to Succeed With People: Remarkably easy ways to engage, influence and motivate almost anyone*. United Kingdom: Capstone Publishing Ltd.

Pausch, Randy and Zaslow, Jeffrey. (2008). *The Last Lecture*. New York: Hyperion.

Petersen, Chistopher. and Seligman, Martin. (2004). *Character Strengths and Virtues: A handbook and classification*. New York: Oxford University Press and Washington, DC: American Psychological Association.

Pirsig, Robert. (1999). *Zen and the Art of Motorcycle Maintenance: An Inquiry into Values*. New York: William Morrow and Company, Inc.

Seligman, Martin E. P. (2002). *Authentic Happiness: Using the New Positive Psychology to Realize Your Potential for Lasting Fulfillment*. New York: Free Press.

Seligman, Martin E. P. (2006). *Learned Optimism: How to Change Your Mind and Your Life*. New York: Vintage Press.

Wiseman, Richard (2004) *The Luck Factor: The Four Essential Principles*. New York: Hyperion.

ABOUT THE AUTHOR

Laura Verrekia grew up in Swarthmore, Pennsylvania. She received a bachelor of arts degree in Psychology from Wesleyan University in Connecticut in 1991 and earned a doctorate degree in Psychology from the University of Pennsylvania in 1996. She currently teaches undergraduate courses at West Chester University in Pennsylvania, including Research Methods, Statistics, Developmental Psychology, and Positive Psychology. She lives in West Chester, Pennsylvania with her three teenage daughters. In her free time she enjoys reading, writing, hiking, and taking creative road trips with her friends and family.

Made in the USA
Middletown, DE
19 January 2018